To Mother in Law

May all your
goose bumps be
little ones.

Love
Cal

Faces of Crime

Douglas P. Hinkle

PEACHTREE PUBLISHERS, LTD.

ATLANTA

To all the men in the Athens, Ohio Police Department—especially Jim Mann, Jerry Elgin, Clyde Beasley and Ted Jones, who have shared with me their hospitality, their war stories, their pool cues and their most sacred Jack Daniel's—this book is respectfully dedicated.

Published by
Peachtree Publishers, Ltd.
494 Armour Circle, NE
Atlanta, Georgia 30324

Manufactured in the United States of America

10 9 8 7 6 5 4 3 2 1

Library of Congress Cataloging in Publication Data

Hinkle, Douglas Paddock, 1923-
        Faces of crime / Douglas P. Hinkle.
            p.   cm.
        ISBN 0-934601-85-2
        1. Hinkle, Douglas Paddock, 1923-   . 2. Police artists—United States—Biography.   3. Criminals—United States—Identification—Case studies. I. Title.
HV8073.4.H56   1989
363.2 '58—dc20
[B]   89-16073
                                                                              CIP

        In Chapter 3 the names of victims, suspects, witnesses and certain others have been changed. Precise locations of offenses and residences are not given, and the identity of the uptown bars where contacts occurred are withheld. In all other respects the events are reported exactly as they happened.

        The material on the five critical distances by the author which appears on pages 192-195 was first published in *Security Management: Protecting Property, People and Assets,* January 10, 1986.

        Material by the author on self-training in observation which appears on pages 195-199 originally appeared as "Invest in Your Memory Bank," in *Police Product News,* March, 1986.

Table of Contents

Acknowledgments

The material for this book was developed over a period of years from my personal experiences both as a forensic artist and, later, as a fully trained police officer assigned to street patrol. It is not often that one who has spent most of his life in the cloistered atmosphere of the classroom and the art studio has a chance to view society from the perspective of the lawman, with hands-on participation in stopping bar fights, containing disorderly mobs, wrestling violent drunks, mediating domestic disputes, entering abandoned buildings at night, or in any of the other police functions, which involve everything from unruly juveniles to murder investigations and the use of deadly force—meaning, specifically, firearms. I don't know when the idea of writing about all this first occurred to me, but early on I started turning out articles for police journals, largely on police art. The notion of a book came later.

It is appropriate to begin by thanking Theodore S. ("Ted") Jones, who, as Chief of Police in Athens, Ohio, had enough faith in me to let me try police work at an age when most cops have already retired. Ted is now Director of Security for Ohio University; he and I still laugh over some of my early mistakes.

Others to whom I owe particular thanks are Captain Clyde Beasley, who taught me more about firearms than I ever learned in the Army, and turned me into a fairly proficient pistol shot; Lieutenant Jerry Elgin, who showed me a lot about making bar checks, repeatedly forewarned me of danger, and probably saved me from serious harm more than once; and Richard ("Rick") Mayer, who succeeded Ted Jones as Chief of Police and authorized my access to many files, records and photographs. My debt to others in that group would require me to cite the entire department roster.

Still others whose generosity with their time and help I can never repay are Sheriff Jim Jones of Hocking County, Ohio; Chief David E. Kelch and Captain Tony B. Wells of the Logan, Ohio Police Department, for making certain records available on the Drugstore Bandit; and Mr. John Ott, Office of Public and Congressional Affairs, FBI, for his help in obtaining photographs of certain terrorists.

I should also like to thank those whose help was indispensable in the preparation of the book itself: Helen Weil, the editor, who has burned much midnight oil in the revision of this manuscript; my longtime friend Phyllis Tickle, Director of St. Lukes Press, who read the original manuscript and recommended it to the examining committee at Peachtree Publishers; and especially my beloved wife Rose-Marie, who typed the manuscript, made many valuable suggestions, and offered the reassurance I often needed.

Introduction

I am a cop. That is to say, I have been for years a certified law enforcement officer, first in Ohio and more recently in Virginia. I *think* like a cop. Cops are my closest friends and associates. "Once a cop, always a cop," the saying goes. But for most of my life I was *not* a cop. I was a college professor of language and literature, especially medieval literature, which is about as far from the real world as you can get.

A lot is made in TV cop shows and elsewhere of the self-imposed exclusivity of cops, the clannishness, and of the almost fanatical loyalty they all feel toward each other, even toward fellow cops they may personally dislike. There is no single explanation for it. Partly it comes from an awareness of the common dangers all cops face daily; from the fact that against those dangers your fellow cops are your only line of defense; and from shared experiences that for many reasons cannot be shared with outsiders.

It comes in some degree from knowing you are part of the Thin Blue Line between those who obey the law and those who break it, between those who need to be protected and those who prey upon them, between civilization and savagery. Perhaps most of all it comes from a gradual but inevitable diminution of the basis for communication with non-cops.

At first a new cop is supercharged with the excitement of new challenges and the belief that he can make a difference. He wants to talk about these challenges with friends and family. But almost immediately he is privy to matters he can't discuss with anybody but another cop. Not even his wife. Sometimes especially not his wife because he doesn't want to frighten or disgust her.

So the basis for communication dwindles and finally crumbles altogether, and the new cop starts going to places where other cops congregate—a certain bar or the Fraternal Order of Police Lodge—where he can speak his mind without having to look over his shoulder first, or choose his words with caution.

For many years I was part of the academic ivory tower, but I was never entirely comfortable with it. Perhaps that is because I had had *some* non-academic experience. I had, for example, been a soldier in wartime. I had worked as a shoe salesman, sheet metal worker, farm hand, hotel clerk. I had lived and worked abroad for long periods among people whose poverty is beyond the comprehension of most Americans. So in retrospect I do not find it surprising that I began to feel increasingly alienated from academia and more drawn to the part of society where the battles are won or lost on the basis of street smarts, rather than coffee lounge repartee in the Rare Book Room.

I was fortunate that one of my good friends was one Ted Jones, Chief of Police, a man with a steel trap mind who reads good books and likes to discuss them. He knew that I had an art background and that once, when I was a student at the University of Virginia, I had done a sketch of a suspicious character. The police had recognized him from it and picked him up, but having nothing to hold him on, they had driven him five or six miles out in the country and told him not to come back. That was in the days when you could get away with direct action.

Knowing these things, Jones one day took me up on my offer to attempt a sketch of a robber from the victim's description. I had no idea how arrogant my offer was, how different forensic art is from conventional art, what a different set of skills it involves.

Inevitably, I was sent through Police Basic, the standard training of the police academy, which I had to do at night because I was still teaching full time. Several months later, after passing the state exams and the firearms qualifications, I put on *the* blue uniform and stepped through the looking glass into another world.

Gradually I was accepted, though the process was slow. Little by little I came to realize that these were the people with whom I identified. My most prized honor came when I, a middle-aged college professor, was given lifetime honorary membership in the Fraternal Order of Police. And when I left Ohio for Virginia, it was my cop friends who showed up to help move the furniture.

I am often asked by outsiders why I have been willing to take the risks of police work for nothing. The question might properly be broadened thus: Why are so many lawmen willing to spend countless hours of their lives, without hope or expectation of reward, pursuing solutions to the insoluble? The answer, if there is one, is probably akin to that of Sir Edmund Hillary on being asked why anyone would wish to climb Mount Everest.

"Because it is there," he said. So is the mountain of crime. Once you have become a cop, you cannot explain your drive to surmount it. Your communication base has eroded and you have entered a secret world understood only by your fellows.

This book is intended to provide a glimpse into one little-known and little-understood facet of that secret world: the police artist—a member of the investigative team and sometimes the only one who can show you what an offender looked like. In the majority of instances the police artist is a certified cop. If you are a police artist very long and you are any good at it, your drawings are going to put some criminals behind bars. Some of them will want to kill you for it.

CHAPTER 1

Murder on Yom Kippur

The night of 5-6 October 1984 was clear and warm, with a hint of autumn in the air. Court Street in Athens, Ohio, home of Ohio University, was filled with milling college students and would remain so until 2:30 A.M., when the bars closed. Some carried paper cups or cans of beer in flagrant disregard for the city's open-container ordinance. The courthouse steps were crowded with young people—a mix of students, townies and latter-day hippies; and on the railing in front of the adjacent Board of Elections office sat a row of young toughs who had come to heckle the students or provoke a fight. A police cruiser circled the block slowly, pausing pointedly in front of the courthouse now and then to underscore the presence of The Law.

At approximately 2:00 A.M. Stewart Mendelson and Peggy Marting, both students, bought pastries and beverages at Carol Lee's Doughnuts about half a block away. They were to be married in the spring. Carefree, they ambled in the direction of the courthouse steps.

Somewhat earlier a local youth named Steve Kempton left the Nickelodeon, a student bar, and encountered his friend John Salyers half a block away in front of the Union Bar. Salyers, who had been released from jail in Florida only ten days earlier and was still wearing his state-issued shoes, was looking for some excitement. They decided to head to "where the action is"—that is, the courthouse. Salyers was carrying two knives. He would only use one.

My phone rang at approximately 2:20 A.M., pulling me out of a profound dreamless sleep. The night dispatcher, Peggy Fortkamp, said to me, "There's been a sort of assault. Captain Beasley wants you to bring your stuff."

I dressed in the dark, kissed my wife on the forehead, and told her that with luck I'd be back for breakfast. I picked up my "stuff," which consists of an attaché case containing an assortment of pencils, erasers, drawing paper and a can of fixative, and drove to the police station.

You seldom see so much blood in one place. It was spattered over the pavement, on the steps, on the door jamb. The doorknob was still slippery with it. Inside, it looked as though someone had taken a bucket of blood and sloshed it at random in great pools on the floor. Crimson strips from somebody's once-white shirt hung in festoons across a wastebasket. Blood-soaked paper towels were everywhere.

"What in God's name. . .some rape," I said. Peggy Fortkamp's euphemistic "assault" was still in my mind.

"It wasn't rape," Lieutenant Dave Cogar told me. "It was murder. A student. He just died."

"What happened?"

"Fight in front of the courthouse. Some guy stabbed him in the neck. He came running over here for help. Romine tried his best, but there was no way to save him. They got him to the emergency room, but he was losing blood faster than they could pump it into him."

"Know who did it?"

"If I knew we wouldn't need you. We got some ideas, of course, because it's usually the same bunch hangs around over there, but can't say which one for sure."

"Anybody see it happen?"

"Oh, yeah. His girlfriend was standing next to him, but she's out of it right now, like a zombie. I mean, she's in shock. She doesn't know any of those guys anyway. She's a student."

"Where's she now?"

"Home, with friends. We'll run down there in a cruiser. Maybe you can get a drawing from her, but I wouldn't bet on it. She's blanked out everything. Doesn't even remember how tall the guy was."

"Anybody else see it?"

"Yeah," Lieutenant Cogar said. "Couple of students from Chicago, but they're not much help. They don't agree on what happened. And there's a little guy named Martello who says he saw it go down."

"Ricky Martello?"

"Yeah," Cogar said. "Know him?"

"Yes indeed," I said. "His father teaches Italian up at the college. I've known the kid since he was born. I would guess he knows all those guys who hang around over there and can probably I.D. whoever did it."

"He claims he only knows one of 'em by name."

"Bullshit," I said.

"Okay, okay," Cogar said. "But all he says is, there were two guys, see, and one of 'em tall and the other one short. He says the short guy is the one that hit him."

"Must have been others who saw it, with all those people around."

"Funny how many of 'em just happened to be looking the other way," Cogar said.

Peggy Marting was indeed out of it. An attractive blonde of slightly more than average height, she seemed unaware of her surroundings or of the presence of others. Either she wandered from room to room in a dreamlike trance or sat staring at nothing. She appeared stunned beyond tears.

I tried to explain what I wanted to do but I got no response. When I asked simple questions she merely wagged her head as if to say I don't know. I asked her to point to one of several stylized geometrical forms on a chart of head shapes. She merely shrugged, an expression of hopelessness on her face.

"All I remember is the knife," she said. "It was about this long, and it had a silver handle that was in two parts, and the blade popped out when he flicked his wrist."

"You mean one of those oriental butterfly knives?"

"I don't know anything about knives, what you call them."

The only thing she remembered about the attacker's face was that he had hollow cheeks.

In such a situation the police artist faces a very difficult choice: on the one hand he wants to respect the victim's need to be left alone to grieve; on the other, he has a very urgent and legitimate need to capture impressions before memory starts to fade. It is not an easy situation for either the victim or the interviewer, who must play each case by ear. I decided to abandon any attempt at a facial description, at least for the moment, and try another route. On the way back to the police station, in the cruiser, I asked her, "Would you like to talk with a clergyman?"

After what seemed a long time she said yes. "I want to talk to a rabbi. Stew was Jewish. We were going to get married by a rabbi. "

"There's one rabbi in town. I'll call his number, but Yom Kippur started last night and he may not answer the phone."

"Please try anyway."

Back on station I learned that Rabbi Grodsky had an unlisted number. He had spent some time in Israel and was a bit paranoid about the numerous Arabs in the student body. I had to scratch my head long and hard before I thought of a member of the Jewish community who would have Grodsky's unlisted number and whom I knew well enough to roust out of bed at 3:00 A.M. on Yom Kippur.

The rabbi was not exactly overjoyed to be disturbed, especially by a goyish cop at such an ungodly hour on such an important High Holy Day; but, given the urgency of the matter, he agreed to come immediately. "A terrible thing," he said.

"I'll send a cruiser for you," I said.

"Sorry," he said. "I have to walk. It's Yom Kippur."

"You can't even accept a ride in an emergency? You're a mile from here."

"Sorry," he said. "It's Yom Kippur. I have to walk."

Rabbi Grodsky did not know where the police station was. It took longer to make sure he understood the directions than it would have taken to bring him there in a cruiser. It was evident that police stations had never occupied a great part of the rabbi's attention.

As I hung up the phone a young man tapped me on the shoulder. We will call him Bill. He was in his early twenties, built like a middleweight prizefighter, and had a quiet self-assurance about him. Although he smelled of beer, he was not tipsy.

"Guy over there says you're the police artist," he said. "I saw the whole thing from about thirty feet and I think I can give you a description."

Talk about luck. The guy was really good, a sharp observer, intelligent, unruffled. As I drew what he described, a face began to form on the paper that corroborated what the girl had told me, especially the hollow cheeks of the attacker.

We were working under the worst possible conditions: the street confrontation had lasted only seconds, the stabbing only a flash; though the new halogen street lights were good, it was not the same as seeing something in broad daylight; and we were doing the actual drawing among a crowd of cops, newspaper reporters, minor university officials, city functionaries, and a janitor who was still mopping up blood. Cameras were flashing, phones were ringing, everyone was talking at once. The table was small to begin with, a fact that was considerably exacerbated by an in-basket of police reports, two ashtrays full of smoldering cigarette and cigar stubs, and the rear end of one large policeman who had chosen the table as the only available spot to rest his weary bones. It was also very late in the wee hours, and I do not do my best art work at such times nor in such circumstances.

Yet, most of the time, those are the sorts of circumstance the police artist works under. He doesn't get to choose the time when crimes go down, nor the type of victim, nor the place where he must work. I have done police drawings in dimly-lit store rooms, basements of police stations, jails, hospital emergency rooms, vehicles, cluttered apartments, even outdoors. Many times one doesn't even have a writing surface to work on; for that reason I keep my things in a flat, hard attaché case that has often doubled as a drawing table across my knees.

But that night, in spite of the noise, the crowd and the glaring fluorescent light, the face continued to emerge. In the process I gleaned a better idea of what actually happened—though what happens in any street scuffle is always unclear to one degree or another, and no two people are going to report it identically anyway.

It appears that as Stewart Mendelson and Peggy Marting passed in front of the line of toughs, one of them later identified as John Salyers made an off-color remark to Peggy, together with a kissing noise. She responded by throwing her beverage at him. He got to his feet and called her a bitch. Stewart, who weighed 250 pounds and favored black leather motorcycle fashions, told him to cool it. Salyers apparently backed down but drew his knife from his rear jeans pocket and fingered it behind his back, out of sight, as he continued to exchange tough talk with Mendelson. (This interval of time, though very short, figured in the prosecutor's decision to go for aggravated murder charge, which involves premeditation.) At that point Salyers' friend Kempton entered the confrontation. Mendelson offered to take both of them into the adjacent alley and "kick the shit outta you." They did not accept. As he turned away, Salyers was at his back; Kempton, who now faced him, punched him in the chest. (This is what Martello saw; his testimony was to figure in the subsequent trial.) Apparently Salyers struck at precisely the same instant, from behind, severing Mendelson's carotid artery. Mendelson, sensing instantly what had happened to him, lumbered around to the police station, seeking first aid. Salyers and Kempton bolted down the dark alley.

It was important to get a precise drawing, not only to expedite the arrest of a murderer but also to establish the identity of the one who wielded the knife as opposed to the one who merely struck the victim with a closed fist.

Two observations are appropriate here. First, the victim of a crime of violence very frequently remembers nothing of the attacker's face, having been too busy staring at the point of threat: the weapon. Second, negative space, the importance of which we will examine shortly, is often overlooked by both victim and interviewer.

In this case Peggy's attention was riveted on the knife; in fact she described a butterfly knife with considerable accuracy even though she had never seen one before and had no idea what it was called. This phenomenon is well known to police investigators and to psychologists. During the so-called "fight-or-flight syndrome," when the presence of adrenalin in the bloodstream is abnormally high, a victim of violence will not only fix attention on the weapon; in addition, peripheral vision will in fact move inward to exclude just about everything else. In this way the victim will perceive the weapon as though greatly enlarged, including miniscule details, but will see only a ghost-like, featureless human form behind it (see Illustration No. 1). This is why Peggy, who was standing perhaps one arm-length from Stewart when he was stabbed, could truthfully state that she didn't notice the features of his killer.

Another element crucial to identification is negative space, which is almost never given the serious consideration it deserves. It is the space between or surrounding the individual facial features, particularly the eyes, nose, mouth, chin, forehead, ears, and under certain circum-

ILLUSTRATION 1   A crime victim often sees the weapon in precise detail but not the offender.

stances, hair. These features are known as positive space (Illustration No. 2).

One of the reasons many police sketches bear no useful resemblance to an offender is that the artist is not trained to ask about negative space. Often he works from a "kit," such as the very popular Identikit®, which is a book of various features and hair types in many different shapes and sizes. The witness simply goes through the book with the sketch artist, reports which variation appears closest to what he or she remembers, and appraises the result when the artist has finished combining them. A more sophisticated kit is Photofit®, which consists of many different photos of the several facial features that can be fitted together to form an infinite variety of faces. The inherent weakness of fixed sizes is obvious. For example, a pair of eyes might be the right shape but entirely too big in relation to the other features. This problem has been overcome by computerized versions such as Comfotofit®, which enables the operator to adjust the size of each feature. Other systems, such as overlays, have proliferated in recent years. They can supply some mechanical skills of police art for departments that don't have their own trained artist, but they all share one insurmountable weakness: human error.

Even the most sophisticated computer can't compensate for three areas of possible error: the memory of the witness, the technical skills of the artist, and the interviewing skills of the artist. Knowing what questions to ask is every bit as important as being able to transform the answers into lines and shadows, and if the interviewer fails to get an accurate representation of negative space, he is licked before he starts.

As an illustration, let's take the distance between the

ILLUSTRATION No.2   These two men have identical features.   Only the distances between the features are changed.

nose and the mouth. In some persons it is very long, in others extremely short. An example of the former would be the late actor Lee Marvin. An example of the latter would be Jimmy Durante, whose nose almost blended into his upper lip when he smiled. If we were to reverse these two characteristics, representing Lee Marvin with Jimmy Durante's short maxillary proportions, and vice versa, we would no longer have recognizable likenesses. That is why cartoonists exaggerate such proportions in their subjects, providing us with identity tags that need no written labels. It doesn't matter how well you may draw Lee Marvin's nose and mouth; if you put them too close together you ruin the impression. That is why I always begin by establishing the head shape and the negative spaces.

This interviewing technique worked particularly well in the case of John Salyers. As Bill, my witness, continued to stress the distances from the cheekbone (zygomatic arch) to the jawbone (mandible) and across the lower face, deep hollows began to appear at the cheek level. This accorded precisely with the descriptions given by Peggy Marting and a couple of others who had gotten a fleeting glimpse of the action. It was the one feature of Salyers' face that everybody mentioned, and its accurate representation caused many of the other features to fall into place.

It was about 3:30 A.M. when I showed the rough sketch (Illustration No. 3) to Captain Clyde Beasley. "Yep," he said to Patrolman Steve Clark, "that figures, all right. Let's go get him."

About that time somebody said to me, "Hey, Hinkle, there's a guy in the other room with a beanie and beard wants to talk with you. I found him steaming down Court Street, sort of lost. Says he's supposed to see the

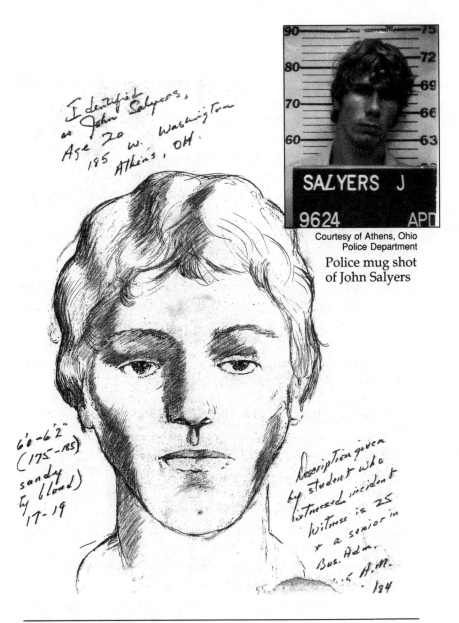

Courtesy of Athens, Ohio
Police Department

Police mug shot
of John Salyers

ILLUSTRATION No. 3 Sketch by the author from a description of John
Salyers, 5 October 1984, immediately after Mendelson was stabbed to
death.

victim's girlfriend."

Rabbi Grodsky peered at me from behind steel-rimmed glasses, looking disconcerted by the unfamiliar surroundings. I introduced myself and ushered him across the hall to the room where Peggy Marting was waiting. "Maybe I can help you get a description of the killer," he said. I thanked him and suggested that for the moment the most important thing he could do was console the girl.

When Rabbi Grodsky emerged he appeared shaken and saddened. A quiet, scholarly man, he was not accustomed to violence and could not quite comprehend its existence, let alone the reasons for it. For him, the exposure to a real-life murder scenario had the effect of a kick in the stomach. Now it was his turn to need someone to talk to, and I was it. We had a long confab right there in the squad room, across the desk where I did the drawing, amid the hubbub and the ringing phones.

It turned out we had something in common: an interest in the medieval poetry of the Spanish Jews, or Sephardim. Years before, I had written a doctoral dissertation on such poetry and published part of it through the American Society of Sephardic Studies. Rabbi Grodsky was patently surprised to learn I had even heard of names like Moses ibn 'Ezra, Todros Abulafia or Yehuda Ha-Levy, men who often poetized in a strange dialect of Old Spanish, using the Hebrew alphabet. We became good friends and remained so for the rest of the time he lived in Athens.

While we were talking, Captain Beasley, Lieutenant Cogar, and Patrolmen Clark and Deardorff left in search of the assailants, whom they were now able to identify as John Salyers and Steve Kempton. They had no trouble finding them. In Salyers' rear pocket they found the silver-handled butterfly knife Peggy Marting had described. It had fresh blood on the blade and in the folding parts. However, because of Martello's statements, the question of which man had done the actual stabbing remained unclear through part of the trial, in the course of which a young female juror fell in love with Salyers and nearly wrecked the conviction (see Chapter 9: Trials and Tribulations).

In this particular case I was very lucky. I had a witness who was not involved in the action and knew neither the victim nor the attacker; he could therefore bring a measure of detachment to his description. He was composed and methodical, with enough self-confidence to correct my lines when necessary. He was an accurate observer who saw the event from a fairly short distance in a relatively good light. And there was only one description to consider since Peggy Marting's was too incomplete to be of value. The result was a drawing that was immediately recognizable to an experienced detective who knew the attacker by name.

I have not always been so lucky. When there are two or more witnesses, both credible and intelligent, who disagree about the basic appearance of a perpetrator, you have an enigma that can't be resolved by merely flipping a coin. That situation is the subject of the next chapter, which addresses the very first police drawing I attempted, in which I made the most basic of all procedural errors.

CHAPTER 2

A Garden Variety Bank Stickup

All the elements were there: a noisy bar, the holiday season, the start of a weekend, and a couple of good ol' boys getting cranked up on a few glasses of suds.

Mark Lewis Wilson, twenty-nine, looked across the table at his younger brother Todd and almost without preliminaries made the simple statement, "I think I'll rob a bank."

The power of suggestion was amplified by the presence of three such institutions within a hundred yards or so of the Cat's Den, where this announcement occurred. Mark Wilson then tore off the cover of a match book and wrote a brief note to be handed to a teller: *Give me all your bills. I have a gun.* They settled on the Diamond Savings Bank, probably because its location off the main drag and at the sharp triangular convergence of two streets afforded the opportunity to escape on foot in any of several directions.

Teller Doris Goldsberry was winding up the day's business when she looked up to see a scruffy man in a Levi jacket with fur collar standing at her booth. He passed her a brown paper sack the size of a lunch bag along with the note, which had been rewritten in block letters on lined tablet paper. His right hand was in his pocket and appeared to be pointing something at her. Startled, she gestured to her supervisor Sally Dailey, who was in the adjoining teller's booth. Ms. Dailey turned in time to hear Wilson speak the only two words he would utter:

"Quit stalling," he said.

Ms. Goldsberry nervously filled the paper bag with bills as Ms. Dailey watched. Both women were standing approximately four feet from Wilson for perhaps a full minute before he took the bag and turned away. He exited by the door opposite the one he had entered, walked through a parking lot, and broke into a run. He was last seen by bank employees as he vaulted a fence in the direction of the Harris Furniture Store .

The bag contained exactly $998, of which $220 was bait money.

The alarm went off in the police station at one minute to 5:00 P.M. on Friday, 11 December 1981—exactly two weeks before Christmas. It was already dark with a raw wind carrying a threat of snow, and I was enjoying the radiant warmth of our wood stove when the phone rang. It was Ted Jones, Chief of Police, calling from the Diamond Savings Bank. There had been "a problem" and two tellers could give good descriptions. Could I meet the investigators there right away and attempt a drawing?

At that stage of my life I was not a police artist, and I knew nothing about forensic art. Some weeks previously, however, Ted Jones had stopped by my house on his way home and had mentioned that he had had to request the help of a police artist from the Columbus, Ohio Police

Department. The problem was, he explained, that the officer had to drive the seventy-five miles to Athens on his day off. The drawing was therefore done after a delay of several days, during which the victim's memory of the offender's face had naturally blurred.

"Ted," I said, "next time something like that happens, phone me. Don't make some poor guy give up his day off."

"You mean you can do a composite sketch?"

"I can probably do as good a job as most of the police drawings I've seen."

Ted looked at me thoughtfully. He takes his police work very seriously and doesn't often act on impulse alone. At the same time he is willing to try experiments— controlled experiments, that is.

After a while he said, "I didn't know you did faces."

He knew about the landscapes and seascapes, because I had exhibited some of my oils and watercolors locally as well as in some large cities. There were even one or two in the room where we were sitting. But because I do relatively few portraits, he had very possibly never seen one by me. He chewed his perpetual cigar as I explained my art background, which had started as a hobby but had developed into an enterprise by which I used to support my family in the summers, selling my paintings along the tourist route in Maine. I told him about studying anatomy, and drawing from live models, and learning the muscle-fatiguing joys of carving in stone. I showed him a sandstone bust of my wife (my first attempt at stone carving) and the head of a prizefighter in marble.

I must have impressed on him that I would really like to make a contribution of time to the community and that I had some of the necessary skills. Although I was confident of my abilities, I was about to receive a very humbling lesson when the phone rang that December evening. I gathered up some pencils and a pad of drawing paper and set out for the Diamond Savings Bank, where I was to make my first major mistake as a fledgling police artist.

That year, 1981, there were over six hundred thousand reported robberies in this country—that is, to employ the FBI definition, ". . . the taking or attempting to take anything of value from the care, custody or control of a person or persons by force or threat of force or violence and/or by *putting the victim in fear*." (Italics mine). Of these, about two percent, or roughly twelve thousand, involved banks. Most of these bank robberies, such as the one at the Diamond Savings, are relatively petty acts committed by unsophisticated hooligans. The spectacular major heists committed by organized crime or trained terrorist gangs, involving millions of dollars, are rare. But big or small, they have one thing in common: in all of them at least one person, and often quite a few, are "put in fear" by punks who take a notion to knock over a bank.

Fear does strange and sometimes terrible things to people. Experience has taught me that when a person in full possession of his or her faculties faces a reasonable expectation of bodily injury or death, perceptions tend to get distorted. Among these perceptions, the height and weight of the offender, as well as general muscularity, are the features most likely to get exaggerated. When two or more people view the same threat, the one most directly threatened is most likely to do the exaggerating.

When you put two such persons in the same room while both of them are still unnerved by the effect of terror, and you try to conduct an interview on the appearance of the offender, you are creating what is sometimes euphemistically described as a volatile situation.

That was the mistake I made on 11 December 1981.

The bank doors were locked when I arrived, but inside all lights were ablaze and people were milling about. I was admitted by a policeman whom I recognized but whose name I did not know at that time. He ushered me into the office of the Director, where I was to do the drawings. There I was introduced to the two tellers. Both were young, intelligent women—pleasant people whose neat appearance and businesslike manner would be an asset to any bank's public image. Both were obviously keyed up, on tenterhooks from their recent fright.

Ms. Goldsberry, the younger of the two, worked with me first because she was the one most directly affected and the one at whom the gun, if in fact there was a gun at all, was pointed. She was still shaking and her voice quavered, for which I did not blame her. She described a man in his late twenties, about five feet ten to six feet tall, weighing perhaps 170 pounds. (These data were at slight variance from those in her written statement.) He had unkempt blonde hair across his forehead, sleepy eyes, straight nose, slightly open mouth, and full facial hair, including mustache and beard long enough "so that you could get a grip on it and hang on (see Illustration No. 4).

Ms. Dailey, the supervisor who saw the subject from an angle, appeared agitated when she viewed the drawing. The hair wasn't right; it should cover the ears. The eyes weren't sleepy enough; the lids should almost cover the pupils. He didn't have a beard or mustache; he merely needed a shave. His jaw needed to be made rounder. His mouth should appear more open and in a sort of sneer, and the teeth should show more. There

ILLUSTRATION No.5 Sketch of Mark Wilson from description by Sally Dailey.

ILLUSTRATION No.4 Sketch of Mark Wilson from description by Doris Goldsberry.

wasn't enough space between nose and mouth. He was only about five feet seven, and weighed maybe 145 or 150. The drawing done from her description appears in Illustration No. 5.

The two sketches do not look like the same man at all.

It must be stressed at this point that the police artist is literally a prisoner of the witness' memory. He cannot argue with the witness, even when a drawing is highly improbable: he didn't see the offender; the witness did. When at the end of the interview the artist asks, "Is this the face you saw, to the best of your recollection?" and the witness says yes, there is absolutely nothing further the artist can do.

The following contrasts between the two drawings reveal just how widely descriptions can vary:

Doris Goldsberry's version	Sally Dailey's version
Head hair leaves ears exposed	Head hair covers ears
Full beard and mustache	No beard or mustache, just stubble
Height 5'10" to 6'0"	Height 5'7" to 5'8"
Weight approximately 170	Weight 145 to 150
Eyes somewhat heavy-lidded	Eyes extremely heavy-lidded
Chin squared off	Chin rounded
Short distance between nose and mouth	Average distance between nose and mouth
Levi jacket with fake fur collar	Blue ski jacket

This illustrates why the first rule of police interviewing is, keep the witnesses from talking to one another until you have finished questioning each and every one of them. Ask them to refrain from discussing the event or comparing notes. Separate them if possible—because, if you allow any of them to get their heads together, one of two things is going to happen: either they will disagree, sometimes violently, or the strongest personality among them will prevail, causing the others to change what might be correct descriptions. In any case, in the immediate aftermath of a crime conflict of opinion among witnesses is bound to be emotional, often intensely so, and this can only hamper the orderly process of investigation.

But I committed the unpardonable error of interviewing both witnesses at the same time because I was not yet a policeman and had not had any professional training in police interviewing or interrogation. The policemen who were present, who could have warned me, refrained from doing so either out of courtesy or because they assumed, incorrectly, that I knew what I was doing. Whatever the case, I ended up with two drawings in which I had little confidence.

As it turned out, both drawings contributed to Wilson's capture. The one based on Sally Dailey's description closely resembles Wilson's actual appearance. Captain Beasley went directly to an album of mug shots and picked him out without difficulty. I was gratified, and a little surprised, at the accuracy of the representation. (Unfortunately, that mug shot is not currently available for comparison.) This drawing gave Beasley a solid idea of whom we were looking for, but it was Doris Goldsberry's description that provided the corroborating evidence necessary to place Wilson at the scene of the robbery.

Wilson remained in Athens for twenty-four hours, during which time he told his brother-in-law Rick Canter about the robbery. For some unexplained reason, he and Canter traded coats. Canter then drove Wilson to Zanesville, Ohio, where he obtained further transportation to his home town of Coshocton.

Captain Beasley, who was well aware of Wilson's family ties to Canter, interviewed the latter at the county jail on 29 December. Canter revealed his knowledge of the Diamond Savings robbery, offering as proof the fur-collared jacket so accurately described by Doris Goldsberry. Captain Beasley obtained the jacket and had it catalogued in the evidence room.

A warrant was issued for Wilson's arrest, and on 5 January 1982, Beasley and Officer Larry Dishong brought him back from Coshocton where the local constabulary had obligingly picked him up. His attempts at an insanity defense fizzled, and he was sentenced to two to fifteen years. Predictably, he served only the first two.

The Cat's Den, where the plan was hatched, no longer exists; its quarters are now occupied by a delicatessen. The Diamond Savings Bank likewise no longer exists; the building now houses a pizzeria. Wilson's $998 loot was not recovered; it figured out to $1.36 per day for his time in prison, small wages by any standards. As for me, my new interest in forensic art was to become an obsession that would literally change my life.

During the next few months I was called several times by the police to do drawings of various suspects: a man who had stolen an expensive guitar from a music store; a youth who used a tear gas canister to rob a convenience store clerk; a burly man who held up a wine merchant at knife point; a teenager who was seen breaking into coin machines; and various others. This whole process had several results.

I learned that most police drawings do not lead to arrests. The ones I did for the Diamond Savings and the Mendelson cases were exceptions. For one thing, it is extremely rare that a police artist comes up with anything approaching a photographic likeness. There is a popular misconception that a police artist sits down with a witness, asks a few questions, makes a few abracadabra gestures with a pencil, and presto, you have a sort of polaroid-camera image of the offender. The cops then take the image out on the street, collar the perp in the nearest bar or floating crap game, and pitch him in the slammer.

That is the stuff of dreams. In reality, more often than not the drawing gets pinned to the bulletin board, where it eventually gets covered up by notices, thank-you notes, wanted circulars from the FBI or U.S. Marshals' Service, and other drawings. However, important ones on major felonies may get reproduced and circulated among other agencies statewide or even nationally.

There are two principal ways in which a police sketch serves the investigative process. First, it helps concretize the facial type, enabling people to visualize what the offender probably looked like in a general way. Second, it saves a lot of time because it eliminates hundreds, and in some cases thousands, of mug shots the witnesses or investigators don't have to wade through. But as a positive identifier in court, the police sketch is next to worthless. No matter how close the resemblance, there will be some differences. For this reason any prosecutor who submits such a drawing in evidence is taking an awful chance that the defense attorney will concentrate on the differences: "My client has a mole on his neck. There's no mole in this picture. Ergo, you have the wrong man. This drawing proves that my client is *innocent!*" And so on, ad infinitum. The drawing is an investigative aid, not a prosecutorial tool.

I found myself spending ever greater amounts of time

at the police station. The more I sat with crime victims and listened to their faltering voices—the more I watched them, male and female, bat back the tears and clench their fists days, weeks, and even months after their victimization—the angrier I became at those who had put them in fear. I am certain that Doris Goldsberry and Sally Dailey will, as long as they live, experience a little stomach-flip when they see somebody who reminds them of Mark Wilson.

That was the year I helped organize a Neighborhood Watch and got elected block captain. I know we prevented a number of crimes because we interrupted a convenience store holdup and broke up a couple of incipient rapes. I began to spend more and more time walking the darker streets and prowling the local alleys—often alone, late at night, with a flashlight and two-way radio. It was dangerous, and I knew it; but I was becoming obsessed with the idea of having a crime-free neighborhood.

But no neighborhood is entirely crime-free. We continued to have problems with graffiti, petty vandalism, drugs. The daughter of a friend of mine was dragged into the bushes and raped.

Then one night there occurred a senseless, vicious beating of an elderly woman who surprised an intruder in the apartment where she lived alone. She survived the attack, but she will never be the same. She was found unconscious, her jaw broken and hanging loose, her face an unrecognizable bloody pulp, several ribs broken and her skull fractured. What made the offense all the more shocking was the fact that she was known as a kind and gentle person, a good neighbor, and a nurse who spent her time helping the sick.

That was when I called Chief Jones and volunteered

for the auxiliary force. Characteristically, I didn't know what I was getting into. We sat and talked about it for quite a while. He had his reservations, and rightly so: I was on the downhill side of fifty, I had no police experience, and, having spent my life as an ivory-tower professor of literature, I probably lacked the necessary street smarts. I countered that I was in excellent condition. (I walked at least five miles every day before breakfast, split my own firewood to heat my house, and worked out regularly on the speed and heavy bags in my son's basement gym). I knew every cop on the force and had taken advantage of the ride-along program available to private citizens.

We finally agreed, but on condition that I take exactly the same basic training as any other police recruit—over three hundred hours of an intensive grind covering everything from courtroom procedure to surveillance to trick driving to first aid, CPR, emergency childbirth, criminal law, you name it. If I got roughed up in hand-to-hand combat exercises with other recruits young enough to be my sons, remember I asked for it. And I would also have to pass the state exams, both the academic side and combat firearms.

"Talk it over with your wife," he said, "and see if you want to invest that much time and energy. Let me know what you decide."

I told Rose what Ted had told me. "It's going to be a struggle," I said. "I haven't been a student for many years. I'm going to have to buy my own police revolver and probably a backup gun, and my own leather and practice ammunition. It'll probably cost me the best part of a thousand dollars. I may get the tar kicked out of me by some of these young bucks I'll have to train with. I'll be on call at any hour, and will probably miss out on some family life. I won't get paid; it's all volunteer. Ted Jones is going way out on a limb for me, because I'm over the age limit. If I fail the exams or mess up on the job, we're both going to get egg on our face."

Rose said, "Do you really want to do this?"

"More than I've ever wanted anything."

"Then go for it," she said.

I had no idea how much I did not know about police work, nor about what goes on in the dark corners of any community.

Specifically, I did not know that a psychopathic rapist had been stalking a pretty young acquaintance of mine. But before I finished my police basic I was to find out—at the hospital.

CHAPTER 3

Psychopathic Rape

The evening of 15 June 1982 I attended my police classes as usual. The subject was the sex offender and his offenses, and the lecturer was Special Agent Howard Linscott, FBI, a recognized expert in such matters. Mr. Linscott is a dynamic speaker who pulls no punches. His audience consisted of all the regular police not on duty that night, recruits like myself, some sheriff's deputies and a couple of University Security people. Some of these men were tough old cops who had seen, or thought they had seen, every hideous thing one human being can do to another. But after four hours of lecture on sex offender profiles and perversions, and slide transparencies of dismemberments, brandings, mutilations and disembowelments, there was not one man present, including the very toughest, who could summon his voice to respond to Mr. Linscott's invitation to questions. I glanced around the room to see a group of men stunned into a trance-like silence. At midnight we arose and filed out. Nobody spoke.

Four hours later, as if by some diabolical irony, pretty Bella Thompson was to begin a terrifying ordeal of torture and dehumanization that exactly matched Mr. Linscott's profile of the psychopathic rapist. She escaped with her life because in spite of the pain and the terror she kept her head, and because some songbirds came to her rescue.

Two days prior to the incident, somebody attempted to enter her dwelling at night but was frightened off by the presence of others and by the barking of her dog. Several people were present. All they saw was a man's arm, clad in a white jersey sweat shirt, appear and disappear at a window. Nobody thought much about it.

For one thing, Bella lived in a house occupied by a half dozen university students—a bohemian mix of male and female, American, Mexican, East Indian—whose acquaintances came and went more or less as they wished, bedding down for a night in any available space including the floor. Often they were identified only by first name or nickname, if at all. There were frequent all-night parties at which liquor, marijuana, and even stronger drugs were known to be used, resulting in complaints by neighbors and repeated warnings by the police. As in many such student gatherings there were numerous casual drop-ins, people never identified simply because nobody cared. The house was the scene of one drug bust that netted a substantial amount of cocaine and the arrest of a student dealer who jumped bail. It was also under repeated surveillance because of the large number of vehicles bearing out-of-state license tags—especially Florida and California—that came and went without explanation.

So the mere appearance of an arm at a window was not considered cause for alarm.

Then, too, Bella's lifestyle added little to her personal security. She drifted with relative ease from one lover to another, none of whom would inspire the confidence of a protective parent. She was a devotee of the uptown bar scene, including one in particular noted for general rowdiness, fights, and the patronage of local ruffians, drug pushers and motorcycle gang members.

Thus Bella could hardly qualify, even within the most generous parameters, as the virginal altar guild type. Her free-wheeling lifestyle contributed in two ways to her subsequent misfortune: first, by breaking most of the safety rules recommended both by the police and by women's advocate groups, she placed herself at the highest risk of violent sex crime; and second, this very behavior pattern made the job of the investigators much more difficult by greatly increasing the number of possible suspects. But be that as it may, what she went through that warm spring night should not happen to any human being. Not ever.

It was about 3:30 A.M. when a muscular white male, whom Bella would later describe as twenty-two to twenty-five years old, paused beneath her second floor bedroom long enough to tie a black bandanna around his face, leaving only the eyes, eyebrows, forehead and hair visible. He then proceeded to cut the telephone lines and ascended cat-like to the porch roof, within easy reach of the bedroom window. He slit the screen with a large knife and climbed through, a process made easier by the absence of a window pane that, broken in a moment of student exuberance, had been replaced only with cardboard.

Bella and her current boyfriend, an asthenic young man named Sandy Campbell, were asleep in a double bed. They had retired some time earlier and had "fooled around" but had not had sexual intercourse because she was having her period. (This fact would be of importance in the medical aspect of the later investigation.) They were roughly awakened by a dark-haired man holding a large knife and a flashlight. He ordered them to turn onto their stomachs and tied their hands behind their backs.

"Wait a minute," Bella said.

"Shut up," the intruder told her. "Just do what I say and nobody will get hurt." He tied the feet of Sandy but left Bella's feet free. Following this, he blindfolded both of them.

"Come downstairs with me," he said. "I'm going to teach you to snub me in a bar."

Some hours later I received a phone call from the dispatcher: could I meet with Officer Bill Green at the hospital emergency room? There had been a rape—a bad one.

I dread rape investigations. They are always among the most difficult of crimes to deal with because you are always on the raw edge of the most intimate of personal disasters, wherein somebody's whole emotional framework has imploded. The task of the police artist is the most delicate of all, in a psychological sense, because he must ask the victim to recall and describe in detail the very face she is most desperate to forget; and he must do it as soon as possible, when the emotional agony is closest to its peak, before memory begins to fade. I always have the feeling I am trespassing, invading an area where I don't belong and am not welcome. Yet it is a task that must be addressed if we, the police, are to identify and isolate the violent sex offender.

When I saw the victim I recognized her face but not her voice. Normally in the lower female register, it was now a high, piping, barely audible squeak that at times faded out altogether. I wondered what horror could have reduced such a street-wise, sexually experienced, self-assured barhopper to a shuddering, whimpering rag doll. No longer the hardboiled young woman of the world, she was now a pathetic little child who needed to be comforted. Her boyfriend, who had been allowed into the room with us, was doing his best; but his best, like the boy himself, was woefully inadequate.

I sat down next to the bed and took one of the girl's hands in mine. "Bella," I said, "do you even feel like giving me a description now?"

She thought a moment. When she spoke, her voice was a hoarse whisper. "I guess I'd better try it," she said, "before I start to forget things."

We began the painstaking process of reconstructing the image of a face half hidden by a bandanna—a task made all the more difficult by two facts: she had been blindfolded for all but a couple of minutes of the two-hour ordeal, and even then her only light had been the indirect glare of his flashlight. Yet little by little, she provided clues that allowed me to piece together an image that aided considerably in the investigation. It allowed us, in fact, to eliminate most of the principal suspects. In this case we were fortunate to make a partial match-up with the mug shot of a known sex offender who lived not far away.

This was possible because, though blindfolded, Bella had been able to postulate the features of his lower face when he forced her to kiss him through the bandanna—features that included a large hawk nose, a bushy mustache and a round chin.

Her odyssey of terror took her from the bedroom down to the dining room, back up to the bedroom, then once again down to the dining room. She was then naked; he had cut off her nightgown with his knife, which she described as a hunting knife with a blue handle and perhaps a six-inch blade. Because it was double edged, I judge it was more likely a military combat weapon. It appears that in the vast majority of rapes, especially psychopathic rapes and lust murders, the weapon of choice is the knife not the gun, for several reasons: at close range a knife is at least as terrifying as a gun; it is more versatile than a gun in torturing, branding, or mutilating the victim; and above all, it is a phallic symbol—a penis substitute, in some cases.

Once down in the dining room the rapist forced Bella to her knees and compelled her to perform oral sex, his knife at her throat. Because she could not do this easily with her hands tied, he cut the bonds. When he failed to achieve orgasm by this means, he ordered her onto her stomach and attempted anal copulation. The examining physician verified that this had occurred, citing trauma and rectal bleeding as evidence.

The rapist repeated his earlier statement: "This'll teach you to snub me in a bar."

"I've never seen you in a bar," Bella replied.

"Don't lie to me."

The man was rough, the pain intense. He kept his knife at her throat. After a while he said, "Let's go upstairs and have some fun with your boyfriend."

Back in the bedroom he untied Sandy's hands, ordered Bella to crawl on top of him, then re-tied Sandy's hands around her back. He commanded them to have sex, which for obvious physical and psychological reasons was impossible. He became agitated, accusatory, threatening: "You're faking, goddammit! Do like I say!" Bella and Sandy, in fear of their lives, went through the motions as the intruder sat on the bed watching and occasionally running a hand over Bella's buttocks. Apparently tiring of this, the intruder ordered her to slip through Sandy's tied arms and took her downstairs again. Once more he attempted anal as well as vaginal sex, neither with much success. This was the point when Bella's real terror began.

The intruder suddenly threatened to amputate a breast. During all the time he had been attempting various types of copulation, he had been running the blade of his knife over her abdomen, breasts, legs, throat. Now he apparently meant business.

"Take your choice," he said. "Your life or a tit." He pinched her nipples and once again said, "This'll teach you to snub me in a bar." Terrified, she begged him not to kill her. He raised the knife as if to stab her, then plunged it into the floor beside her.

Laughing he said, "I think instead I'll heat this in the kitchen and brand you." He got up and took a couple of steps toward the kitchen.

"No, please. . . ."

Once again he laughed. He ordered her onto her hands and knees and made her crawl around in imitation of a dog. Once he commanded her to bark. Again he said, "This'll teach you to snub me in a bar." Repeatedly he would threaten to amputate a breast, poking at her flesh with the point of his knife. Repeatedly he would appear to change his mind.

"Say your prayers," he kept saying and then, laughing, "No, I think I'll wait a while."

Bella began to fear she would go insane and strove to keep as calm as she could. She tried to talk to him in a low voice but could not get him into a dialogue. He suddenly said, "Spread your legs," and with the blade of his knife began to cut her pubic hairs. He was rough, pulling on them as he sawed.

At that point he deliberately inserted first the handle then the blade of his knife in her vagina. "You like that, don't you?" he said.

"It hurts. Please. . . ."

He then dictated to her the sounds he wanted her to make—ejaculations of pain alternated with moans of pleasure.

She had an inspiration. "Is that birds I hear? I think it's getting light."

The intruder listened for a minute to the first robins and bluejays of the dawn.

"Oh shit," he said. "I gotta get the hell outta here." At the back door he paused long enough to say, "It's been a fun two hours, baby," and then, "If you go to the police or I see any cops around here I'll come back and kill both of you. Adios."

I am convinced that, given another half hour of darkness, he would almost certainly have killed her. Everything he did fit the buildup to the classical lust murder.

Bella continued her description: unkempt straight black hair that seemed to spring out from the rapist's head in various directions, parted more or less in the middle; deep dark eyes that bored into her with the intensity of branding irons; eyebrows that arched upward to form sharp triangles as he glowered; deep frown wrinkles; and a forehead of more or less average height. These features are depicted in Illustration No. 6. Once, when he forced her to kiss him, she was able to run one hand over the surface of the bandanna and took note of

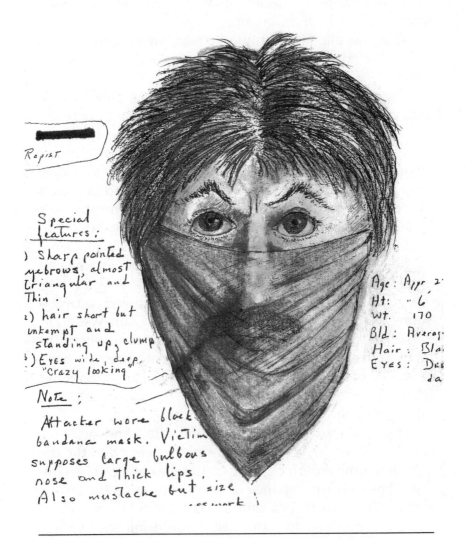

ILLUSTRATION NO. 6 Sketch of rapist from description of victim. Note she was able to postulate shape of nose and mustache by sense of touch.

the large aquiline nose. It was obvious to her he wore a thick, bushy mustache and that his chin was rounded more like a girl's than a man's.

That was all. His stature, she said, was about five feet eleven or six feet tall and he weighed perhaps 170 pounds.

The drawing is not very satisfactory as police drawings go, but incomplete as it is, it still enabled investigators to eliminate most of the original suspects—the many males who frequented Bella's address. In that sense alone, it saved a lot of time. But it had additional value. That afternoon it was shown to bartenders and bouncers in the numerous uptown bars. In two of them—the two Bella frequented most—it struck pay dirt. Yes, one bartender said, a man resembling the drawing was in his bar the day before, but he didn't know the subject's name. He would try to find out if the man returned.

The field of suspects was soon narrowed to two: a young man from a small town near the Ohio-West Virginia border, and a resident of the same area where the rape occurred. The former was eliminated on the basis of a footprint that didn't match. The latter, whom we will call Mike Mahoney, turned out to be very interesting indeed.

Mike, it seems, lived down the alley and across a couple of backyards from Bella's place. He fitted the description almost perfectly: the features were close to identical. The only discrepancy of significance was the fact he was a good two inches shorter than the 5'11" or so that Bella had ascribed to him. But considering the average two-inch exaggeration we have noted as common among crime victims, Mike Mahoney fell within the parameters. Moreover, it seems he had a record. He had done hard time in a couple of state prisons for a number of sex crimes. Officers investigating previous offenses had found bondage equipment, including chains and studded black leather apparel in his quarters, as well as stacks of pornographic literature and photographs. Furthermore, he had been seen in the proximity of Bella's house and was quite possibly the subject seen by the bartender in her favorite watering hole.

But all of this is not enough to establish the probable cause necessary to convince a judge to issue a search warrant. It is entirely speculative. The pictorial image is incomplete, and the rest could be coincidence. As to the footprint, even if a match-up were made, any defense attorney would quickly—and correctly—point out the impossibility of determining when it was made. Although investigators combed the house and retrieved hair and fiber trace evidence, none of it was any better than the footprint without a match-up. Even the two pubic hairs that Bella spat in the sink when she brushed her teeth would at that time have identified only the gender and racial type of the owner. With today's DNA "fingerprinting," which permits precise identification from hair as well as other cells, the result of this case might have been very different.

Bella was out of the hospital shortly; her physical injuries were limited to some small cuts and bruises, and the anal trauma. The real damage was psychological, manifested almost immediately in an anxiety bordering on paranoia. Because she had gone to the police in defiance of the rapist's orders, she feared he would keep his promise to kill her. She thought she saw him following her wherever she went. Consequently her cooperation with the police became increasingly tenuous, to the point that investigators began to suspect she knew him but was afraid to identify him. She turned from an essentially likeable if somewhat hardboiled young woman into a scared rabbit. After a few days she packed up and left town for good.

Authorities on rape generally identify three types: anger rape, power rape and sadistic rape. There is clearly much overlap among these categories. Some, such as Bella Thompson's, manifest elements of all three.

Sadism of the type Bella Thompson suffered reveals careful planning and preparation (such as the severed telephone lines) and is generally associated with a perpe- trator of above-average intelligence in contrast to the schizophrenic rapist, who, though often just as brutal, is characterized by greater spontaneity and lower intelli- gence. The psychopathic rapist-murderer chooses his weapon (most frequently a knife) in advance whereas the schizophrenic grabs anything handy (often a bludgeon such as a baseball bat, tire iron or heavy rock). The psy- chopathic rapist prolongs the act over a considerable pe- riod of time whereas the schizophrenic tends to get it over with quickly.

While there are many exceptions to this profile, Mike Mahoney's crime that night was a classic example of psy- chopathic rape. Mike Mahoney is quite intelligent, the son of well-educated professional people. His aggression was an erotic act that sought gratification by inflicting pain and in dehumanizing the victim. It was clearly pre- meditated and involved bondage as well as voyeurism, piqueurism, sodomy, fellatio, ritualism and penis substi- tution, most of which are illegal. Branding was at least threatened. Souvenirs (pubic hair) were taken. The as- sault lasted an estimated two hours. The violence was intentional and involved specific sexual injury to the victim. A phallic symbol (knife) was used to torture. The suspect used obscene and abusive language. Much of the act was bizarre and ritualistic. The risk of lust murder was clearly present. It is a textbook example of the psychopathic rape that often immediately precedes such a murder.

It was not long before this intelligent loner, unmarried and without any known girlfriends, perceived he was under surveillance and took up temporary quarters with relatives as a cover. Although the investigation continued for some time, detectives failed to uncover enough concrete evidence to take to a grand jury.

The investigators are still convinced there is only one person who had the opportunity, the motive and the ability to commit the crime, as well as a knowledge of the neighborhood and a previous record of similar offenses: Mike Mahoney. They feel they know this, but knowing something and proving it beyond a reasonable doubt to all twelve jurors are two different things.

Likewise, closing a case and proving guilt are two different things. For example, if a known murderer dies in a shootout the case is simply closed. Similarly, if investigators despair of ever finding enough evidence to convict, the case goes to the inactive file or may be closed altogether.

This case is in the inactive file.

Mike Mahoney is still free. There is evidence he may have returned to the scene of the rape on one occasion: one of Bella's housemates came back from class to find her contraceptive gear scattered over the floor. Nothing else was touched.

Although from the strictly investigative standpoint the value of the sketch of Bella's attacker is clearly less than that of John Salyers or of Mark Wilson, it did serve three investigative purposes: it eliminated a dozen or so initial suspects; it established that the rapist was probably seen in a bar frequented by Bella at a time when she was there; and it matched in several particulars the features of a man whose police record and known behavior pattern squared with the offense in question.

Although Mahoney is still at large, new scientific procedures have allowed detectives to consider reopening the investigation.

CHAPTER 4

Making Money Sketching Hoodlums

In the week following the Bella Thompson rape we recruits struggled through a forbidding battery of topics that were certain to appear on the state exam for police certification: indicators of mental illness and alcohol abuse; local narcotics investigations; gambling and vice; liquor law enforcement; and mob/riot control. The entire week after that was devoted to handling domestic disputes—the second most deadly threat to the life of a policeman. Every evening at 5:30 I would gather up my notebook and pocket tape recorder and head for the classroom. Every night between 11:00 and midnight I would return exhausted but exhilarated. During the daytime I studied, hiked, chopped wood, punched the bag, practiced pistol marksmanship. I even built a pistol range in our huge basement (it measured sixty feet in length), using heavy logs and over a ton of sand as a backstop. Soon I had to take up reloading my own ammunition to cut down on the expense.

Once my wife said to me, "Look, I don't mind the .22 and I can take the .38 all right. But please, when you're going to fire the .45 down there, let me know so I can plan to go shopping or something."

The practice was having its desired effect, though: my times were getting faster and my groups smaller.

Police marksmanship is different from traditional competition in which you align yourself at right angles to the target, aim carefully, and take your time before squeezing the trigger. This is the pattern of the Olympic competitions, for example. But police pistol shooting is geared to the notion of fast-moving street combat, and everything is done under very strict time constraints. You are given a certain number of seconds to fire a specific number of rounds at a man-sized target, at varying distances of up to twenty-five or even fifty yards. The average distance at which a police shootout occurs is twenty-one feet, or seven yards. The most difficult exercise for me consisted of the following: at seven yards you are given four seconds to draw your weapon from the holster and put two rounds in each of three upper-body silhouette targets placed ten feet apart. That's not four seconds per target, it is four seconds *total*. At my age I always had to pressure myself to make the four-second limit, but I have seen young men with athletic reactions do it in less than three.

I also continued to practice sketching. I wore out a lot of pencils that summer, and ruined a lot of good drawing paper. I practiced. And practiced. And practiced. I drew with charcoal, pencils, pen-and-ink. I sketched everything in sight—my wife, my children, visitors, stray dogs, trees, the mailman, neighbors. I filled whole trash cans with crumpled paper, and of course it all paid off in greater economy of line and a freedom of style that is generally at variance with the tight, two-dimensional stiffness of most police drawings.

The terms composite drawing or composite sketch are often used among policemen synonymously with police sketch. The reason for this is that most police sketches are put together from many different images of different parts of the face. The witness examines three or four pages of noses and selects the most likely one; the policeman then copies this onto a sheet of paper. The same procedure is repeated with other features: eyes, mouth, ears, eyebrows, and so on. In that sense the result is truly a composite.

This procedure is often necessary because most police departments, especially the smaller ones, do not have a trained artist on the force, and for perfectly good reasons the commanding officers do not usually wish to involve a civilian artist in the investigations. They are therefore often stuck with a copying job that is flat, stiff and awkward, the subject appearing to stare at the viewer full-face, expressionless. This is unavoidable, but unless a department has its own trained artist, it is the best that can be offered.

From the beginning I have avoided such prepackaged systems, preferring to do a drawing as a whole, not as a "composite," and depending on my own knowledge of anatomy, light and shadow, and three-dimensional perception derived in large part from my training in sculpture. Consequently the forensic drawings I have done cannot really be called *composite* sketches.

There is an additional problem in police art: you are drawing something you have never seen. It is one thing to draw from a live model posing on a dais in the center of a classroom; it is quite another to draw a face from the description of a witness who may be distraught, terrified, wounded, exhausted or half-drunk. This brings into play

the other half of police art, just as important as draftsman-
ship: interviewing. If you can't elicit the information you
need, if you can't pull the witness into a cooperative ven-
ture, your drawing will probably be worthless.

One of the best examples of this I can remember involved the rape of a seventy-eight-year-old woman. I
was riding patrol when the dispatcher called me to the
sheriff's office. The victim was being brought in just as I
arrived. Supported on either side by her daughter and
son-in-law, she appeared unsteady and badly shaken.
Her face and arms were bruised, her eye blacked. She
had just come from the hospital where she had been
treated and released. She was clearly overwhelmed by
the enormity of what had happened to her: a large black
man, weighing over two hundred pounds, had knocked
on the door of her rural trailer; when she answered, he
quickly shoved her into the bedroom, clamped a pillow
over her face and raped her. What little resistance she
was able to offer only gained her some bruises. She
seemed quite unable to speak. She had never been in a
police station of any kind, and I am sure she was terrified
by the presence of uniformed officers. Furthermore, she
was clearly overawed by the presence of a real honest-to-
John *artist,* who was himself an authority figure. Who
was she to tell him his lines were wrong? I tried to explain to her that my eraser was as important as my pencil—that *she* was the boss because she, not I, saw the attacker. It didn't work.

"Ma'am, what did his nose look like?"

Silence.

"Did it look like this?"

"I guess so."

"Or was it flatter in here?"

"If you say so."

I was getting nowhere. Both her daughter and son-in-law tried to convince her: "Mama, you've got to help the man or he can't help *you*."

Silence. After a while I excused myself and went to the sheriff. "Bob, this drawing's no good. The poor old thing won't correct my lines. She's still scared stiff, and to make things worse, she thinks I'm some kind of wizard."

The drawing is included here as an example of an effort that failed miserably. (See Illustration No. 7).

The offender was caught, however, because an attendant at a nearby gas station became suspicious and noted his appearance as well as the company name on the van he was driving. He was arrested in Columbus, Ohio, and was tried and convicted—an exception to the usual conclusion of such cases.

A poor interview will produce a poor likeness, but sometimes there is nothing you can do about it. Except, as the bard said, "sweet are the uses of adversity." Failure can be turned to advantage, and that's what I did. Over the course of the summer I was involved in a number of similar cases in which the victim/witness could not provide a decent description because he/she

—had been looking at the weapon, not the face.
—was scared silly.
—didn't know what to look for.
—couldn't assign priorities to the things seen.

The problem was compounded, I believe, because in most instances the police investigator

—wasn't trained in the type of interviewing
  needed for a good facial description.

ILLUSTRATION NO.7 Vincent Tracey according to description by rape victim.

—didn't have adequate knowledge of facial or cranial anatomy to ask meaningful questions.

—was often no better at assigning priorities than the victim/witness.

What was needed, it seemed to me, was a *system*.

At that time our crime prevention unit offered, once a year, a training session for the employees of the city's several banks. It was a pretty sophisticated program that included a mock robbery staged by advanced drama students and semi-professional actors under the dynamic direction of Professor Dennis Dalen of the Ohio University drama department. It is a very realistic and convincing presentation—so realistic, in fact, that many of the tellers are genuinely frightened when the actors enter brandishing real guns, firing blank cartridges and barking harsh commands peppered with street language.

I decided I could piggy-back it. Chief Jones and the bank officials liked the idea: I would prepare a training program of two to three hours' duration and present it to the tellers a week or so before the mock robbery. Afterward they would write descriptions of one or more of the robbers. One teller would be assigned to do a police sketch with me.

I worked on the program for months. Because classes were once again in session at the university I had to work entirely at night, often until 2:00 or 3:00 A.M. This meant, of course, that professional scholarship got put on the back burner.

By November the program was falling into shape. The lettering was finished, the mug shots collected, the drawings completed. A local photographer with an oversupply of outdated film and a sympathy for law enforcement agreed to do the slides for fifty cents apiece.

Around the first of December I issued an invitation to a small group of people for a preview. Present were a prosecutor, a defense attorney, a bank official, two or three detectives, Chief Ted Jones, a judge, and several others interested in various aspects of crime. But my baptism of fire came through an invitation from one of the detectives present, Captain Clyde Beasley. Clyde is a master sleuth and a dedicated cop—so dedicated, in fact, that he organized the Southeast Ohio Intelligence Group, an association of professional lawmen representing a wide variety of agencies. Once a month the members—local police, sheriffs and their deputies, FBI agents, state highway patrolmen, IRS investigators, coroners, prosecutors, game wardens, forest rangers—meet to exchange information, report offenses and request assistance. It is a highly skilled and very knowledgeable group of professionals.

When Beasley asked me to show them my program I was both flattered and scared. I began by telling them that with practice all you need is one glance at a face in order to be able to describe it later, in all its essentials, to a police artist; and that the other half of the equation is that the artist or investigator must know what questions to ask. I showed them the principle of negative space and pointed out the five critical distances in any face (see Illustration No. 8). I showed them a chart of different head shapes (see Illustration No. 9) and underscored that this is the most basic of all questions in a police drawing. I talked about basic geometrical forms and how they apply to different types of features: foreheads, noses, eyes, mouths. And I emphasized that no face is in perfect balance; for example, sometimes one eye is larger than the

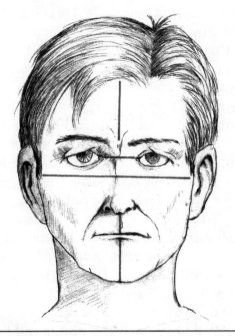

ILLUSTRATION NO.8 The five critical distances on any human face. A
mistake in reporting any of them can ruin a likeness.

SOME HEAD SHAPES

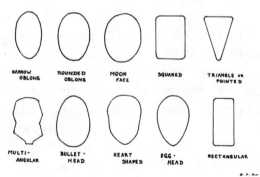

NARROW
OBLONG

ROUNDED
OBLONG

MOON
FACE

SQUARED

TRIANGLE or
POINTED

MULTI-
ANGULAR

BULLET-
HEAD

HEART
SHAPED

EGG-
HEAD

RECTANGULAR

ILLUSTRATION NO. 9 Ten basic head shapes.

other. One of the prettiest girls I ever saw—a Latin beauty—had one eye noticeably higher than the other.

I talked in this vein for an hour, using the slides I had prepared. At the end of that time some of them remained to ask questions.

One of them said to me, "You know, you should get this program marketed. I'll bet it would sell good."

About that time I wrote an article on observation in which I incorporated some of the ideas basic to my program and sent it off to *Police Product News*, now called *Police.* Several months later they published it under the title "Invest in Your Memory Bank." A large advertisement of Syndistar, Inc., publishers of training programs in slide, video and movie format, appeared on one of the pages of text. I sent a copy of the article with the ad to Syndistar in New Orleans and described my training program in greater detail.

Not long after that I received a phone call from Ralph Behrman, Syndistar's marketing manager. Could I catch a plane to New Orleans? They would like to get a first-hand look at my program, with a view to adding it to their offerings.

Syndistar offered me a contract, but the whole program had to be reworked to bring it into line with commercial standards. It took a long time—many months of selecting and rejecting, organizing and refining. The number of slides grew from the original eighty to over one hundred and fifty, so that the program had to be split into two parts. It finally hit the market in the summer of 1987 under the title "How to Remember Faces, Parts I and II." It has since sold to well over three hundred police departments across the country.

Meanwhile, I was continuing to do police drawings of

criminal suspects. The file folders were beginning to bulge. I was being called to neighboring cities and towns. When that happened, Chief Jones would simply put me on loan, as it were, and I would take an unmarked cruiser. It was good PR for our department and good practice for me.

One of the cities calling me with increasing frequency was Logan, Ohio, situated about forty-five miles southeast of Columbus. I have done drawings for them on cases ranging from strongarm robbery to rape to aggravated assault.

I had heard rumors of a bandit who preyed especially on drug stores over a four or five-state area, a professional bad-ass who wore an automatic in a shoulder holster and carried out his robberies with military precision.

I did not know he was at that very time planning to knock over a drugstore in Logan, nor that I would eventually meet him face to face in a shoot-out.

CHAPTER 5

The "Drug Store Bandit"

I finished my police basic course on 15 July 1982 and took the state exams the same day. I did not consider them easy, but somehow I passed. That was all that counted. I had already passed the firearms qualifications with revolver and shotgun—not brilliantly but at least more than adequately.

For a while my participation in the law enforcement process was confined to the city of Athens, with an occasional walk across Court Street to the sheriff's office in connection with one or another offense that occurred out in the county. My salaried job continued to be the teaching of language and literature at Ohio University. Yet whenever I had the time, I put on the blue uniform and rode shotgun with one of the patrolmen. And whenever a call for a drawing came through I would grab my kit and set to work.

It wasn't long before word began to circulate throughout southeast Ohio, and I started getting requests for assistance from nearby towns. As I mentioned, one of the towns that began to ask for my help with some regularity was Logan, Ohio. On one particular occasion I was to interview a pharmacist who had been held up at gunpoint the day before by a lone bandit.

I was met by Chief Steve Barron of the Logan Police Department, who ushered me into a fairly spacious conference room and gave me the background on the offense. The previous evening a lone gunman had entered Risch's Drug Store, across the main drag from the Hocking County courthouse, just before closing time. He had approached the pharmacist, a young woman named Jolynne Evans, and opened his jacket to reveal a handgun in a shoulder holster. He demanded drugs and cash. With admirable presence of mind she said to him, "Let me clear the store and close up, so nobody will panic. Then I'll get what you want." She moved down the aisles with calm efficiency, announcing closing time and ushering customers and the two remaining employees onto the street, locking the front door behind them. She then returned to the pharmacy section at the rear, where the gunman gave her a list of the specific drugs he wanted.

"He was very businesslike," she would say later. "He knew exactly what he was after." He disabled the telephone, told her to remain in place for ten minutes, unlocked the front door and left.

"Gutsy girl," I said. Barron agreed.

At that point in our conversation a uniformed officer knocked and admitted Ms. Evans. She was an attractive young woman in her late twenties, of average height with fairly short blonde hair, bordering on pretty, and she exuded an air of quiet self-confidence that made her calmness in the presence of an armed robber seem quite believable.

It is my custom to spend a few minutes talking with a witness before attempting a drawing. Ms. Evans spoke freely of the experience, describing the robber as a large man about forty with a bushy mustache and glasses. She estimated his height at six feet and his weight at two hundred pounds, which turned out to be right on target. I instinctively liked her and found her both forthright and intelligent.

But finding somebody likeable and intelligent is no guarantee you'll produce an accurate drawing together. An hour or so of sketching, erasing, and sketching some more produced only the image in Illustration No. 10. Comparison with other drawings of the robber will show that it has practically no resemblance to his actual appearance.

There were two problems: first was the hair, which in Illustration No. 10 sticks out like a mane in all directions. This is not terribly important because hair styles can be changed quickly and easily and are therefore not reliable as identifiers. But the second problem was basic and inescapable: the mouth. Ms. Evans kept repeating, "He had a strange mouth. The lower lip was very heavy." I made the lip heavier and heavier until it looked so grotesque I had to thin it down again. We compromised on the version here, which is wrong because of the misrepresentation of two facial muscles. "It's just not right," Ms. Evans told me, "but I don't know how to tell you to correct it."

The Drug Store Bandit, as he came to be known, got away with a substantial haul that included some five hundred Dilaudids (which in some metropolitan areas had a street value of up to $40 per pill) and 450 Percodans, as well as Preludins, Demerol, Valium, Nembutols, Placidyls and Biphetamines. Some of these were for the bandit's personal use. The rest, when converted to cash, would constitute a pretty substantial payday.

ILLUSTRATION No. 10 Alfred Hastings, from a description by Jolynne Evans.

We later learned that Alfred Hastings, the Drug Store Bandit, was a multi-state offender with warrants out against him from Illinois to New Hampshire. At the time of the incidents in Athens, Ohio, we did not yet know his identity. But we did know that his M.O., or *modus operandi*, was remarkably similar to that of an armed bandit who had pulled several recent stickups in neighboring counties. He would stake out a target drugstore to learn its interior layout, the identity of the personnel and the make, color and model of the manager's automobile. He would park his own car at a considerable distance, usually in a parking lot, and proceed on foot to the objective, usually just before closing time. He would quietly display his weapon—a semi-automatic pistol in a shoulder holster—to the manager, pharmacist or clerk in charge and make his demands in the form of a "laundry list" of controlled substances and cash. He would then obtain the key to the manager's car and fix the hands of his victims behind their backs with tape, clothesline or cheap handcuffs. Following this, he would drive the manager's car back to where he had parked his own, get in his car, and depart. Although he had no record of firing his weapon at anyone and seldom had to go beyond displaying it in its holster, he gave his victims the impression that he was quite prepared to do so.

The Prescription Shop is the very first business you encounter as you turn into the shopping mall on West Union Street in Athens, Ohio. It has ample parking space both in front and on the side as well as across the drive. It is easily accessible, that is to say vulnerable, and can be observed at leisure from a wide choice of angles. West Union Street affords escape not only in the east-west direction but also by various cross streets and by a state route that feeds directly onto a four-lane highway to Columbus. The Prescription Shop was made to order for Al Hastings.

He hit it on the evening of 20 May 1985, just before closing time. Characteristically, he chose a moment when there was nobody in the shop except the pharmacist-manager and his wife, who also worked there. The M.O. he employed was identical to that of the Risch Drugstore robbery in Logan—with one major exception. In that case he had not bound the hands of Jolynne Evans at all, but at the Prescription Shop he handcuffed both Mr. McAllister and his wife. (The handcuffs he used were cheap things that would not respond to standard police handcuff keys and had to be removed with bolt cutters.) True to form, he took the manager's car keys and drove back to his own car, which he had left in the parking lot of O'Bleness Memorial Hospital half a mile away.

He got away with his usual laundry list of drugs and some cash.

I met the McAllisters at the police station. It was pointless to separate them because they had already had plenty of opportunity to compare notes. The best I could do was to interview them one at a time for separate drawings, using a desk at the far end of the investigations section for a measure of privacy.

Mrs. McAllister went first. Like Jolynne Evans, she was puzzled by the conformation of the robber's mouth and had difficulty describing it. She was far more concerned with his hair style, which she insisted on describing in great detail.

I have had this experience on numerous occasions. It presents a diplomatic problem to the forensic artist because if he drags the witness away from one aspect in order to examine another, he may alienate that witness and end up with a useless sketch. Yet he must observe priorities. Basic facial bone and muscle structure cannot be changed short of major surgery; hairstyles can. But naturally witnesses want to concentrate on what interests *them*. It was hairstyling that interested Mrs. McAllister, no matter that if and when we caught up with the robber he might have changed his hairstyle or even had his head shaved. When I finished the sketch from her description, I knew it was worthless. Although it shows some similarity to the drawing from Jolynne Evans' description, it is too pretty to be believable (see Illustration No. 11).

I proceeded to Mr. McAllister, a relatively young man with some knowledge of anatomy and a scientist's penchant for precise detail. He noted several such details not mentioned by the other witnesses—for example, a point on the tip of the nose where the bilateral alar cartilages meet. He also noted the development of the corrugator muscle, which attaches to the nasal part of the frontal bone and draws the eyebrows together, producing a frown. But most important, he solved the riddle of the "strange mouth."

Surrounding the human mouth there is an oblong muscle, the *orbicularis oris* (sometimes called the kissing muscle), which attaches to several others. One of these is the *depressor anguli oris*, which begins on the lower jaw near the chin. Its function is to draw the angle of the mouth downward at the corners. In Hastings this muscle is exaggerated, giving him a permanent dour scowl (see Illustration No. 12).

While I was doing these drawings the investigators called the Logan P.D. to advise them we had just had a robbery with the same M.O. as the Risch Drugstore inci-

ILLUSTRATION No.12 Alfred Hastings, from a description by pharmacist. Note downturned mouth and frown wrinkles.

ILLUSTRATION No.11 Alfred Hastings, from a description by Mrs. McAllister. Note unrealistic ornate hairdo.

dent. By this time Logan had been able to obtain mug shots of several possible suspects whose M.O.s matched up, who were not then in prison, and who could have been in the neighborhood. Two Logan P.D. officers jumped in a cruiser and brought these photos down to us. They arrived as I was finishing the drawing based on Mr. McAllister's description.

The matchup with Hastings was both obvious and immediate. We now had a prime suspect identified by name, prison serial number, reputation and M.O. However, having a suspect and capturing him are two different things. Hastings was to remain free for another two weeks before he went to the well once too often.

Chapter 6

The Dormitory Rapist

Police drawings, we know from experience, are seldom if ever any good to the prosecution. Such a drawing will never be an identical likeness because the memory of the witness is never exact. Consequently a defense attorney will concentrate on any deviation from photographic reality, exaggerate it, and turn the sketch to his client's advantage. Thus a police drawing is valuable only to the pre-trial investigation.

However, when two or more witnesses produce similar independent images of an offender, even when a considerable interval has elapsed between drawings, there is usually enough overlap to convince investigators they're looking for the same person.

A couple of rapes that occurred back to back in 1987 provide a striking example of how this principle works. About 2:00 A.M. on a cold February morning, a college student named Jenny Walker (pseudonym) closed her textbooks, set the alarm clock for 7:00 A.M., and set about getting some rest before a test scheduled for the following noon. She was awakened by the presence on her bed of someone she assumed to be one of the girls who shared her apartment. Because all the residents of that unit were lesbians, she did not at first react with alarm. It was only when she became aware that the other person was holding a hunting knife to her buttock that she realized it was not her current lover.

The intruder forced her to roll onto her back, at which time she caught a brief glimpse of him in the darkened room and perceived that he was black. However, she was not wearing her glasses and was able to make out very little else. He covered her eyes with a hand; when she tried to remove it he became angry and said, "Don't look at me." He pressed the blade of his knife against her vagina, uttered the curt command, "Spread your legs," and proceeded to rape her vaginally. When he tried to kiss her she noted a mustache. She also noted his height (five feet seven or five feet eight), his deep voice, the odor of cigar smoke, and the fact that he cut the phone line. Before he left he took five dollars and a fistful of change from a glass jar.

I attempted a drawing later that day at the police station but was very dissatisfied with it (see Illustration No. 13). The victim was not especially cooperative and made a poor witness. Officer (now Lieutenant) Jerry Elgin took the drawing and scoured the mug shot books. He came up with one possibility, a long shot who, it turned out, had a rock-solid alibi.

A little over three weeks later began a bizarre series of events that left another girl raped, still another murdered, several people terrified, and one offender behind bars, probably for life.

It is a liberal orthodoxy that cops don't give a hoot about rape victims. Based on my years of experience, I would say that this is not only false, it is about as unfair a

Code 48
Suspect
B/M
Age 36
5'11" – 6'1"
175–185

By #36
2/4/87

Light skin
(coffee w/cream)

Witness says this
is a strong likeness.

ILLUSTRATION No. 13 Unsatisfactory sketch of anonymous rapist from description by uncooperative witness.

piece of slander as I could name. We are the ones, along with the social workers and the psychiatrists, who have to deal with the mental anguish, the weeping, the distraught relatives, the outraged husbands and fathers. More, we are the first responders so that it is we who have to deal with the initial impact of this terrible crime—the shock and often the injuries and the blood—before the ambulance or the support groups arrive. We are the ones who, along with those support groups, view the social devastation that rapists leave in their wake: the disrupted lives, the long-term depression, the wrecked marriages and yes, the occasional suicide.

That is why we don't hear cops making jokes about rape. At least I have never heard one do so, and I have covered more rapes than I can remember. Rape is *never* funny. If you want to learn something about it, sign up for a ride-along with your friendly neighborhood policeman and you may get a chance to respond to one. If so, don't be surprised to learn your cop friend favors the death penalty for rapists.

Elsie Williams (pseudonym) was not consciously inviting violence when she neglected to lock her door before retiring. Regrettably, this is often a sort of standard operating procedure among college students still affected by the commune mentality of the Sixties; and university security people have found there isn't a whole lot you can do about it.

Thus, she awoke at 4:30 that morning to find a black male in her dormitory room. She ordered him out of her room and followed him to the lobby area on that floor to make sure he left. That was her second mistake. He turned, pulled a hunting knife, and ordered her back into her room. Holding her with one arm and pressing the blade of the knife against her neck, he said to her, "Do what I tell you or you'll get hurt." He then proceeded to rape her. As in the Jenny Walker rape, he did not remove his clothes but merely unzipped his fly. Adding to her terror, the assailant retained his knife, stabbing the pillow by Elsie's face rhythmically as he committed the assault.

On this occasion he was more talkative, even voluble, though he spoke mostly in a low voice or a whisper. He told her that his name was John, that he was from out of town, that he had been drinking, that he held a doctoral degree, and that he was looking for his girlfriend, whom he called Joyce. After the sexual contact with Elsie, he showed her a picture of "Joyce" and remained to talk a while. He took down her phone number, dormitory and room number, and asked her for cab fare; when she denied having any money he left.

Elsie waited until she was fairly certain he had exited the area before she went to the room of her friend Billy Welch (pseudonym), a rather feckless youth who lived on the same floor of her co-ed dorm. Welch spent the next few minutes comforting her before going to the room of the Resident Assistant, another student named Tom Quigley (pseudonym). While Welch was pounding on Quigley's door, a black male whom he later described as about five feet seven, 130 pounds and in his late twenties, emerged from the adjacent stairwell.

"What the hell's all the racket about, man?" he asked. "Something wrong?"

"My friend Elsie's just been raped," Welch replied.

"You mean Elsie that lives down the hall here? I know her. Maybe I can help."

At that point Quigley emerged, listened to Welch's report, and told him to go back to Elsie's room and wait there while he went for the Resident Director. The black male accompanied Welch. When Elsie responded to the knock, she took one look and cried out, "That's him! That's the man that raped me!" At that point Quigley joined them.

Incredibly Welch, who towered over the assailant and outweighed him by perhaps forty pounds, merely said to him, "Now you just leave. Just go away. Go-o-o!"

This happened as Quigley was approaching. Here were two young men nearly six feet tall and weighing at least 170 pounds apiece, and one offender at five feet seven and perhaps 130 pounds; yet neither student made the slightest move to detain him. Whatever the explanation for this faint-heartedness, the suspect was allowed to walk off unimpeded and simply disappear. This was later to cost an innocent girl her life.

I was called to the hospital to attempt a drawing later that morning. I met with J. R. Ator of University Security, who was investigating the case. He introduced me to Elsie, a short, very plain and somewhat overweight blonde. She was still badly upset, giving way to intermittent weeping, and was obviously not in any condition to collaborate on a police sketch. After conferring with Cheryl Cesta-Miller, a rape crisis intervention specialist I had worked with on previous cases, we agreed to postpone efforts at getting a description until that afternoon, at which time the medical examinations would be completed. Meanwhile I would attempt a drawing from the description of Billy Welch. It is included here as Illustration No. 14. One can immediately see some major differences, especially in basic bone structure, between this and the previous drawing (No. 13) from the description of Jenny Walker, who saw the assailant only in the dark. I

D/M
Age 21-24
Ht 5'8"
Wt. 130-135
Complexion brown
short hair
no scars or
marks.

Code 48
2/26/87
#36 APD

B/M
age 24?
Ht. 5'8"
Wt. 130-135
Complexion
dark brown,
short hair
no scars or
marks

Description
by victim

Code 48
2/26/87
By #36
APD

ILLUSTRATION No.14 Sketch of Dixon from description by victim's friend.

ILLUSTRATION No.15 Sketch of rapist later identified as Michael Dixon from description by victim.

had already concluded that her drawing should be discarded; I felt that her classification of it as a "strong likeness" was motivated by a desire to get the whole business over with as quickly as possible. In contrast to the devastation felt by most rape victims, her compelling emotion seemed to be a general misanthropy directed largely toward males.

That afternoon I talked again with Elsie, who, in the supportive presence of Ms. Cesta-Miller and her assistant Sally Mykal, attempted to cooperate on a sketch. She was still too emotional to be able to help and the effort was once again postponed. On our next attempt, she was still severely shaken and subject to sudden unpredictable bursts of crying, but she made it through the ordeal. Although there are certain superficial differences between her rendition and that of her less-than-lionhearted friend Billy Welch, the two drawings are clearly within the same ballpark. They were published side by side in the Ohio University *Post* on 2 March and in *The Athens Messenger* the following day (Illustration No. 15).

On 27 February, the day after the rape of Elsie Williams, an Ohio State co-ed named Lisa R. Heitkamp returned to her apartment at 1494 North High Street, Columbus, some seventy-five miles away. This is a student residential area where unlocked doors and a generally free-wheeling lifestyle are the norm. As she entered, she surprised a black male in the act of burglarizing her quarters. He shot her in the face with a .38 calibre revolver, killing her instantly. He then broke into another apartment, where, according to *The Columbus Dispatch*, he forced two residents to accompany him to a bank money machine where he withdrew $300 of their money, then vanished. Columbus police, checking their files, noted that a Toledo man named Michael Dixon, who was a jail inmate currently living in a Columbus halfway house, fitted the description given by the two victims of the bank machine robbery. When he failed to return to the halfway house the police figured, correctly, that they just might find him in Toledo.

Meanwhile an Ohio University student named Michael Kennedy, then living on Mill Street in Athens, saw the two drawings in the O.U. *Post*, gulped, and called the police. "I think I drove that guy to Columbus," he stammered.

Mill Street is a student housing area where, like Columbus' North High, open doors and a bohemian way of life prevail. It was early in the morning of 27 February when Kennedy heard a noise on the stairs. Already dressed, he poked his head out his door to see a smallish black man coming up.

"What are you doing here?" he asked.

"Man, I got a friend name of Joe lives here, I think. I'm looking for Joe."

"Nobody named Joe lives here."

"I gotta get to Columbus, man. Joe was supposed to drive me, I gotta be back in class on time."

It happened that Michael Kennedy had to go to Columbus that day. To this perfect stranger (who was in fact inside the house in violation of the law and under most suspicious circumstances) he said, "I'm going to Columbus. You can ride along if you want."

The intruder wanted. For the next hour and a half he bent Kennedy's ear with his tales of woe—especially his "fight" with his girlfriend, whom he now called Mary. (O. U. Security had checked and found that no "Joyce" existed at the dormitory Elsie's attacker had mentioned earlier.) Kennedy's statement to the police reads, in part,

He said he had hit Mary out of anger and that some-
one had called the police. He said he needed to get
out of town until Mary calmed down. I didn't know
whether to believe him or not, but as I said before I
had no reason not to. I couldn't dis-believe [sic]
him just because he was black or something. How-
ever, when I saw the sketches in the Post, I figured
the man was the same one who raped the girl. [The]
name and address that the man gave me is Mike
Frank, 13th Street, Apt. #B1, this is in Columbus
just off High Street.

Police from the two jurisdictions quickly put two and
two together. The address mentioned by Kennedy's passenger was just around the corner from the apartment of
the murdered girl, Lisa Heitkamp. The drawing done
from Michael Kennedy's description appears as Illustration No. 16.

Dixon, whose mug shot appears as Illustration No. 17,
was picked up in Toledo and returned to Columbus. A
twenty-count indictment, including the murder charge
with death specification, allowing the jury the option of
requiring execution, was laid on him. Elsie and two witnesses travelled to Columbus where, independently, they
gave positive identification of Dixon in an in-person
lineup as the dormitory rapist. (Jenny Walker, the victim
of the 2 February rape, declined to cooperate at that time.)

Dixon pleaded not guilty to two counts of aggravated
murder, five counts of aggravated robbery, two counts of
kidnapping, two counts of receiving stolen property, two
counts of having weapons under disability and seven
lesser counts. It was also learned that he had done hard

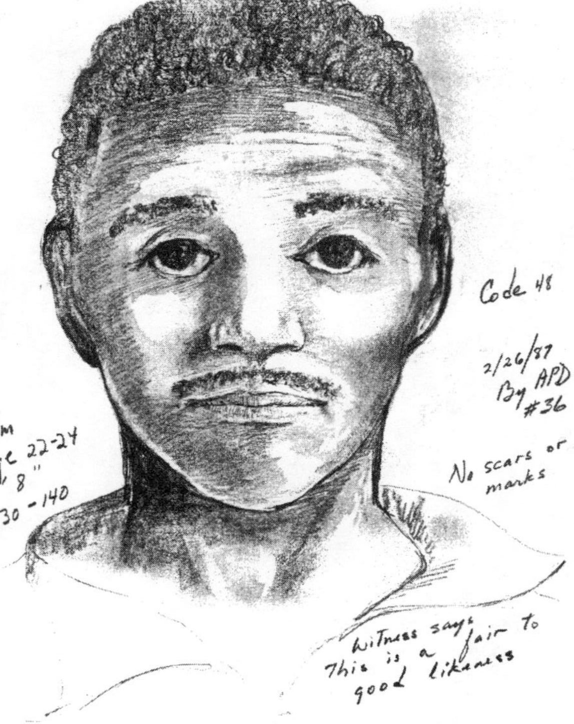

Courtesy of the Franklin County, Ohio Sheriff's Department.

ILLUSTRATION No.17 Police mug shot of Michael Dixon.

ILLUSTRATION No.16 Sketch of Michael Dixon from description by Michael Kennedy.

time as far back as 1976 for rape and aggravated burglary.

Because he was convicted in Columbus on several of the charges, including murder, and was sentenced to a total of 132 years, Athens delayed prosecution; but if at the end of the 132 years (or probably much less) Dixon is still alive, a couple of Athens cops will no doubt be there to greet him as he totters out of prison.

The two sets of crimes in two widely separated jurisdictions might never have been associated in the minds of law enforcement officers had it not been for the two forensic drawings seen by a college student named Michael Kennedy. It was his willingness to come forward that enabled us to pin down Dixon's identity and to close the case—hopefully—for the next 132 years.

CHAPTER 7

The Police Artist as Investigator

A major problem in law enforcement stems from the high premium that is necessarily placed on the security of information. Confidentiality and secrecy are not only a way of life, they are indispensable to the success of the whole. In many instances they are indispensable to the continued existence of the officer, of an informant, or of a key witness.

For this reason cops are a close-mouthed bunch. Information is imparted on a need-to-know basis only. Cops generally do not discuss the details of any case with outsiders. You may have noticed that when you ask a cop about a certain sensational crime, he will probably tell you, "I'm not working that case. I only know what I read in the papers." He may actually be telling you the truth, but chances are good he's merely observing the code of common sense. He doesn't know where the information he gives you will end up. It could cost him—or somebody else—his job or even his life, and he's not willing to take that chance.

This tradition exists even within a given police department. Unless you have a good reason to know—a special legitimate interest—your fellow cop will probably not volunteer much information, if any, about the cases he may be privy to. And in the absence of such a reason, you don't ask. Often this necessary secretiveness can present a number of problems, such as normal human sympathy. Let's assume you respond to a complaint by neighbors of a domestic battle and you find three people: a mother and father, both fighting drunk, and a frightened child. You take proper steps to assure the child's safety, and later you want to know how it's getting along. But subsequent investigation has revealed sexual abuse by the father. Unless you are directly involved in that investigation this is clearly none of your business.

Curiosity can become a problem as well. Let's assume this time you're the first car to roll in after a bank robbery. You will be followed immediately by the investigators (in a large department by the robbery detail) and by the resident FBI agent, and your duties will be perfunctory. The investigators will not go into detail with you because investigation is *their* job. Yours is to secure the area, remain as long as you are needed, and then go back to patrolling the streets. You may notice later that when you pass those same investigators in the hall, they will clam up until you are out of earshot. This is not because they don't trust you; it is simply a time-honored standard practice to safeguard the security of information. The fewer people who possess a given piece of intelligence, the smaller the chance it will get leaked.

You may feel your status as first responder ought to entitle you to the privilege of sharing follow-up knowledge of the investigation. Not so; the public safety comes first. (This is a principle not understood by many news hounds, who feel that their press card entitles them to know *everything*, NOW, and the public safety be damned. They do not have a good track record for respecting confidentiality and have consequently blown the cover off many a criminal investigation. The result is a natural tension between law enforcement and the media.)

The reverse of this concept is that the investigators want as much input as possible from the street cops. A mountain of tips may labor and bring forth only a mouse, but that's better than no mouse at all. But, unless the street cop understands the status of the investigation, he can't know whether something is worth reporting or not. In some ways, the situation is analogous to that of a group of people each of whom possesses a different piece of a treasure map. Without all the pieces, you can spend a lot of time digging in vain.

This concept took me a long time to get accustomed to. Time and again I would be called to do a drawing and then hear not another word about it. At first this bothered me because once you are called to work on a case, you develop a natural interest in its progress and eventual outcome. What I did not understand is that once my particular skills were utilized, my usefulness to that case was at an end. Nobody was under any obligation to involve me further; in fact, to do so would be wasteful and even counterproductive.

So I learned to do my drawings, go back to what I had been doing before, and ask no questions. Nowhere was this lesson clearer than on those occasions when I was called off patrol to do a drawing—that is, asked to change hats during the course of a shift. When that happened, I was participating in the law enforcement process both as a street cop and as an investigator. Under such circumstances it is hard to divorce oneself from the subsequent investigative process; but tempting as it may be, you have to control the urge to butt in.

I remember, for example, one bitter January night in 1984 when I was riding patrol with Bill Green and we were called to a local hotel to answer a larceny complaint. An experienced con man had worked out a clever routine: he would knock on a guest room door, identify himself as one of the maintenance crew, and ask permission to check the plumbing. He wore workman's overalls and carried a couple of wrenches for stage props. Once inside, he would tap on a pipe and then ask the occupants to help him by going into the bathroom to operate the fixtures—run the shower and/or the lavatory, flush the toilet, etc. While they were thus occupied he would rifle their belongings.

On this occasion he victimized a family of three: mother, father and college-age son. He kept up a running chatter of instructions to them, thanked them politely for their help, bowed and left.

The father was the first to discover his loss, a wallet containing cash and credit cards. The mother was missing her jewelry, which included a valuable emerald as well as her diamond engagement ring. The boy lost some cash.

The theft was reported so quickly the hotel management thought the perp might still be on the premises, but they had no such luck. Because both male victims had seen him up close and could give descriptions, I went back for my drawing kit and set to work right there at the hotel.

The father attempted to give me a description, without much success. He had noted very little about the man, and his attempt to describe what he did see was totally inept. The only features about which he was certain were the man's physique (very tall, perhaps six feet six, very skinny) and his race (black). "He didn't *look* like a black man, but I can't say why." After a few minutes I gave up and pitched the drawing in the waste basket.

The son, by contrast, was very precise about what he had seen. I worked with the kid for perhaps an hour, until he said he could remember nothing else. We then showed the drawing to the father.

"Jesus, yes, that's him all right."

The father's problem was anthropological, but his son went right to the heart of it. Normally we associate the concepts black person or Negro with the racial stocks originating in West, Central or South Africa. These peoples are characterized by broad flat noses, protruding foreheads, and thick lips of more or less equal dimensions. But the stocks originating in East and Northeast Africa have abutted for many generations on lands occupied by peoples of Semitic or Arabic origins, and there has been a lot of gene flow, resulting in "black" people with thin lips, knife-bridged noses, and foreheads that do not bulge but recede slightly. This was apparently the racial origin of the offender here (see Illustration No. 18).

The father looked at his son and said, "You did a good job. We'll probably never see our money again, but let's hope we get your mom's jewelry back."

I turned the drawing over to the investigators and went back to riding patrol. Nobody said another word about it to me until the man was caught near Cleveland a few weeks later, partly on the basis of the drawing. Neither the jewelry nor the money was recovered.

There is a difference between solving a crime and clearing a crime, though the distinction is fairly subtle. A

Description by John Parker (son) Jan. 20 '84

Black male with light complexion badly acne-scarred

Age appr 25

Ht 6'6"

Very thin

John says this is an accurate image of subject. D.P.H.

ILLUSTRATION No. 18   Hotel room con artist from description by victim's son.

crime is solved when the identity of the offender is established; it is cleared when a final disposition is made so that the files may be closed. This may come about through the arrest of the offender for that particular offense; or for another offense in another jurisdiction; or through his or her death or through recovery of stolen goods or a kidnapped person, etc. In other words, when you solve a crime you know who did it; but knowing this doesn't by itself clear the case. Police chiefs talk about their clearance rate, which is what counts. An additional category, "Clearance by exceptional means," is employed by the FBI to identify those cases cleared because the complainant decides not to prosecute. An example would be a stolen car complaint dropped because the owner discovers the vehicle was borrowed without his knowledge by a friend.

That is one of the reasons behind Captain Beasley's Southeast Ohio Intelligence Group. Where many criminals operate over an area encompassing several jurisdictions, cooperation among agencies is essential to the clearing process. The sharing of information is vital.

A police artist who is on call to more than one jurisdiction in the same geographical area is in an excellent position to make contributions to more than one department's clearance rate.

In December 1984 a man we will call Jack Miller was transporting about $3,000 of his employer's money to the bank when he stopped for gas at a station on Athens' Richland Avenue, a main artery through town. At the parallel line of pumps was an older model pickup truck with much orange primer paint, driven by a large man who was accompanied by a slightly built boy of perhaps eighteen to twenty. Miller paid for the gas and returned to his truck, at which time he noted that the zippered bank pouch containing the $3,000 was still on the seat beside him. When he turned the key in the ignition, he realized his battery was dead.

When he got out his jumper cable, the big man in the pickup came over and offered to help him. Now Miller was an ex-cop and should have known better than to leave the money pouch on the front seat, but that is what he did. He also allowed the stranger to start the engine out of his view behind the upraised hood. The big man then got back into his pickup truck and was quickly swallowed up in the heavy Richland Avenue traffic. The money pouch, of course, was gone.

Jack Miller gave me a very good description of both subjects. The big man was in his late twenties. His face was moon-shaped with a heavy double chin. His hair was long and covered his ears, and he needed a shave. He wore an old dark-colored toboggan cap (see Illustration No. 19). His young companion had a longish face, very soft, with nothing but peach fuzz on it. He was slight, almost frail, with straight blond hair parted in the middle, that fell to his shoulders (see Illustration No. 20). An androgynous type, he seemed shy and apparently did not take an active part in the theft. Nothing further was said, and after a while I forgot the incident.

Nearly a year later I got a call to Hocking County on an armed robbery. On the evening of 16 November 1985 Ethel Moore (psuedonym), age thirty, returned to her rural home after dark to discover a strange van parked in her driveway, with a man at the wheel. Going inside with her two young sons, she found herself in the midst of a robbery in progress.

Some minutes earlier Betty Taylor (pseudonym), her

ILLUSTRATION NO. 19 From a description of a thief by victim who lost $3,000 in cash.

ILLUSTRATION NO. 20 Thief's young male companion. Note androgynous nature of features.

seventeen-year-old stepdaughter, had responded to a knock at the front door. She held her baby in her arms. "Who is it?" she called out.

"I'm a friend of your dad's."

As the girl opened the door she was confronted by a young blond man who pushed her down and pointed a gun at her face. His companion, a large, dark-haired man, held a shotgun to her as the blond one began to search the other rooms. The big man ordered her to lie down as he unzipped his pants. At that point the baby began to cry loudly, so he ordered Betty to go into the other room and sit on the floor. She asked him to get her a baby bottle, which he did. Meanwhile he was issuing orders to his younger companion, urging him to "hurry up, we gotta get outta here."

At that point Mrs. Moore opened the front door to see the large man standing over her stepdaughter with a shotgun. He told her and her two small sons to lie face down on the floor and not look at him.

"Where is your husband?" he asked.

"I don't know."

He shoved his shotgun against the back of her neck and shouted, "Lady, I said where is your husband?"

"I swear I don't know."

He poked her wrist with the muzzle of the gun and said, "What's that?"

"My watch. I'll give it to you."

He took it, along with her purse (containing over $500 in cash), her credit cards, passport, driver's license, and miscellaneous other items. He yelled once more to his companion to hurry up. After they left, the women, the baby and the two boys stayed on the floor until they heard the van leave the driveway and head east.

I did the drawing of both suspects from the descriptions given by the seventeen-year-old Betty Taylor. (Although Mrs. Moore disagreed with the drawings, she declined to participate in the sketch process on the ground that she had not gotten a good look at either face.) The large man, who seemed older than his young effeminate companion, is shown with a full beard and wild uncombed head hair, quite curly, sticking out in all directions. He has no mustache. This is the point on which Mrs. Moore disagreed; according to her, he had a full mustache as well as beard. The importance of the drawing is that it served as a basis of comparison to a previous rendering; the basic bone structure and the shape of the visible features—eyes, nose, mouth, eyebrows—are remarkably similar to those of the man who stole Jack Miller's bank pouch a year earlier. Moreover, a year is ample time to grow a full beard such as the one shown here (compare Illustrations 19 and 21).

That much, of course, could be coincidence. But let's take a look at his young companion: he was blond and slight of build and had somewhat soft features like those of a girl. In a word, he is—like the companion of the big man who stole Miller's money—androgynous (compare Illustrations 20 and 22). The eyes, eyebrows, nose and mouth match quite well; the hair is approximately the same length. If the face in Illustration 22 seems a bit older, remember that a year had passed. As these coincidences grow in number, so does the mathematical possibility that we are looking at the same pair of offenders. Given the androgynous nature of the younger man in both cases, we begin to suspect a homosexual "husband-wife" relationship.

Some three weeks after the Moore robbery, an elderly

ILLUSTRATION No. 21 Robber, from description by 17-year-old female victim. May be the same man as in Illustration No. 19.

"SAM"

Logan
Code 50
11/16/85

Logan
Code 50
11/9/85

w/m age 21
5'8" - 5'9"
140 - 145 lbs
blond straining hair

ILLUSTRATION No.22 Robber's young male companion. May be the same person as in Illustration No.20.

ILLUSTRATION No.23 This young man, who robbed an elderly homosexual, may be the same person as in Illustrations No. 20 and 22.

man living not far away was robbed and beaten with the stock of a shotgun. He nearly lost an eye, but agreed to give me a description soon after the offense. His speech was slowed and hesitant, and he seemed confused—not surprising in a man who has just been clubbed about the head with a gunstock and who can't see out of one eye. However, the drawing I did from his description once again shows marked similarities to Illustrations 20 and 22—especially the eyes, eyebrows, nose and mouth, as well as the general elongated shape of the face and head. Although he was wearing a toboggan cap, the victim described his hair as long, blond and stringy (see Illustration No. 23).

A reasonable person would begin to suspect, despite the superficial dissimilarities between any two of the drawings, that we have a fair matchup between the Athens and Logan cases. Add to this the fact that this last victim (now deceased) was a well-known older homosexual whose fondness for young men and even boys had previously brought him afoul of the law, and our suspicions about the sexual orientation of the younger man in the Miller and Moore cases begin to harden.

I turned the drawings over to the Logan authorities: Sheriff Jim Jones and Police Chief Steve Barron. But I also made photocopies and turned them over to Captain Beasley in Athens, who was immediately struck by the similarities.

Although he and other investigators have their suspicions, no arrests have yet been made. However, it is important that the similarities between the faces in Athens and Logan would never have been noted in the normal course of investigations; what brought them together was the intervention of a forensic artist who just happened to work on three cases separated by thirty-seven miles and three police jurisdictions.

CHAPTER 8
Unexpected Paths

I was riding patrol with a young cop named Brent Bobo when the call came over the radio: "Code 50 in progress, Super-X Drugstore on East State." Here it comes, I thought, armed robbery. Bobo tramped on the accelerator and flipped on the bar flashers as I unsnapped my holster. I am not much of a church-goer, but I remember crossing myself. In that kind of situation you'll take all the help you can get.

When the radio transmission came through we were patrolling the uptown student grog shop strip, about two miles from the mall where the robbery occurred. As we screeched onto East State Street we heard the voice of Chuck Mains, the dispatcher: "Subject took key to manager's vehicle. That'll be a small silver Honda, Ohio license RGB-918."

When I heard these words I began to suspect the Drug Store Bandit; taking the manager's car matched his known M.O.

As it happened, Lieutenant Dave Burnette, the shift commander, was patrolling that end of town. Proceeding east, he heard the announcement as he was approaching the main entrance to the mall. He immediately spotted the Honda as it moved through the parking lot toward the stop light at the intersection of the mall entrance and East State Street. Burnette drove past the Honda, verified the license number, then did an abrupt U-turn to fall in behind it as it accelerated rapidly westward on East State. "I've got him ahead of me inbound," we heard Burnette say. By inbound he meant headed toward downtown. That meant Bobo and I would at some point meet or pass them.

A few minutes earlier—just before the 10:00 P.M. closing time—the robber had entered the store and walked directly to a back room, where he pointed a gun at Kenny Kasler, a clerk who was assembling a barbecue grill. He then marched Kasler into the main part of the store, where he confronted Dan L. Hudson (the store manager and owner of the Honda) and the other employees. He instructed them to close the store, which they did. A customer's attempt to enter the locked door upset the robber for a brief moment; and when one of the clerks, who had not seen the gun, made a smart remark to him he drew it from under his shirt and asked, "Do you know what it's like to be shot?"

Other than that, he was calm. "He was very courteous," Hudson said. "He didn't rush us too much."

As usual, he produced a shopping list of drugs. Those supplied to him included:

cocaine	*valium*	*morphine*
amphetamines	*codeine*	*dysoxyns*
dilaudid	*barbiturates*	*seconals*
opium	*demerol*	*percodans*
dolophine	*percocets*	*tylox*
quaaludes	*ritalin*	

He also took between $600 and $700 in cash. He then handcuffed one employee, binding Hudson and the other two with tape. He took the keys to the Honda, told them not to move for ten minutes, and let himself out. As he left he said, "If the police are out there I'll come right back in and we'll have a shootout from right in here."

Hudson quickly worked his hands free and phoned the police.

Bobo and I were rapidly approaching the mall area. As we sped under the Route 33 bypass and past a string of shops we spotted the Honda with the police cruiser right behind it. We heard Burnette say, "He's turning into Hardee's." Burnette wheeled in after him, and our cruiser turned left to follow. We pulled to a screeching halt with our front bumper within inches of Burnette's cruiser.

Using the door for cover, I rolled out with gun drawn as Bobo did likewise. The robber had jumped from the Honda holding a gun in his right hand and a paper sack in his left. He ran behind a car, where all but his legs were obscured from my view by a tree. At this moment he raised his gun and aimed at Burnette, who fired first. I saw the man drop from a distance of perhaps thirty feet. He landed face down, his pistol skittering a foot away from his outstretched hand.

Bobo and I ran up to cover him. Burnette stood at his head and called, "Can you hear me?"

"Yeah, I can hear you."

"What's your name?"

"Hastings."

"That's the guy," I said, "that's wanted for the Logan holdup and the Prescription Shop, too."

"Keep him covered," Burnette said. "His voice doesn't sound like he's hurt too bad. One of you call the emergency squad."

Hastings' gun was in plain view. It was a Smith and Wesson 9mm semi-automatic, fully loaded with a round in the chamber, the hammer back and the safety off. Subsequent search revealed he was carrying a total of fifty-six rounds, some of them in spare clips. He was prepared for lethal combat.

What we did not know at that time was that this professional bandit had done his homework right under our noses. He had entered the city parking garage where the police cruisers not in actual use were normally parked and had memorized which ones carried shotguns. He later boasted that he was ready to "take out the windshield of any cruiser with a shotgun, and any cop behind it." Given a reasonable angle and distance, his 9mm would have done the job. Our cruiser carried a shotgun.

The emergency squad rolled in and began their examination of Hastings before transporting him to the hospital. I nearly wept when they cut off his beautiful Bianchi shoulder holster with a huge pair of scissors, ruining it.

Incredibly, he was not badly hurt. Burnette's .38 slug had entered the chest and had made an exit wound in Hastings' back on what appeared to be a direct line through the heart—a perfect killing shot. Yet here was this man, not only *not* dead, but fully conscious and as mean as a rattlesnake with a hangover.

What happened, we learned, is that Burnette's .38 slug had struck the edge of a disposable lighter in Hastings' shirt pocket, glanced off it, entered the skin, and skirted the rib cage to exit in the back. Ballistics is a strange science full of surprises. Those things happen.

Consequently a shot that would ordinarily have killed him merely sent Hastings to the hospital for a quick patch job. That same week the Chief began proceedings to change the issue weapon from the relatively ineffectual .38 special to the vastly more authoritative .357 magnum, which doesn't pay much attention to cigarette lighters.

About that time two other cruisers showed up, driven by Officers Lyons and Clark. Bobo and I could have returned to routine patrol, and probably would have, had not a large, fat and slatternly woman run from the bar across the street—The Maplewood Inn—to summon help.

"Turrible fight over there," she said. "Two guys a-carvin' each other up with bottles." Bobo and I ran to the front door, which was beginning to disgorge excited spectators. Inside we found two men in a face-off: drunk, bloody and fighting mad. The bar was jammed, the shouts deafening. I don't know how we talked them apart or got them outside, but we did.

With them came two women, their wives. One was very pretty. Both were about ten thousand years higher in the scale of evolution than their husbands. I have never understood why attractive women will sometimes marry bums like that, but they do. In this case the women were the *force motrice* behind the combat. The two men, it seems, had each been married to the other's wife. In the bar they had begun a bragging contest about what each had done with the other's present wife in the privacy of the bedroom—what, with which, to whom. As the boasts became louder and more graphic, and the cheering of the other patrons more unrestrained, tempers flared. Nobody seemed to know who hit whom first, or with what, but it had to be one of Athens' better donnybrooks of recent times.

Outside, Bobo took the smaller of the two men aside. I got the big guy. He was built like a series of cubes stacked one on the other, with legs like fireplugs and no neck. When I took his arm it felt like a locust fence post. I doubted I could even get handcuffs around his wagon-tongue wrists, even if he would hold still.

He wouldn't. He took a notion he didn't want to go with me, and there was no way in God's world I could make him without recourse to what's sometimes called "excessive force." In some communities you might get away with dusting him off with a nightstick, which I was not carrying anyway, but in Athens it is considered bad manners for the police even to chide a prisoner in a well-modulated voice. I doubt I ever would have gotten him cuffed and in the cruiser without the help of six by-standers who by this time were afraid of him and wanted him gone.

"Where you takin' me, pig?" he yelled from the prisoner's cage.

"First you're going to the hospital to get sewed up," I said. "You're cut bad. Then you're going to jail."

For the rest of the drive to the hospital the interior of the cruiser was filled with a cascade of obscenities the likes of which I hadn't heard since I went through infantry basic under a leather-lunged master sergeant down in Texas, back in the Second World War. I could even have admired this guy's style, the richness of his metaphors and the fluidity of his delivery except that he was so utterly foul mouthed and I was the object of it.

There comes a point at which the most self-contained of us has had enough. Even a sociologist has been known to lose his temper with a dunderheaded student, or a judge to strangle a promiscuous wife. My point of no return came when I got this musclebound oaf inside the emergency room.

"Ain't nobody gonna sew me up," he yelled. "Any nurse or doctor try to touch me, I'll bust their goddam fucking face open." At that point I experienced a cold rage I have never felt before or since. I stepped in front of him, took my heavy four-cell flashlight off my belt, and held it up to him.

"You see this?" I said. "I am going to take the handcuffs off you because that's the only way we can get your hand sewed up. But if you try to take a swing at anybody—nurse, doctor or anyone else—I am going to take this flashlight and part your hair clean down to your asshole. Do you read me?"

It was not approved procedure, but it worked because it was the kind of approach he understood. He was relatively docile as we led him to one of the several rooms off the main hallway of the E.R. section. The trouble was, it was a busy night. All the rooms were already in use by patients, mostly college students who had fallen down, wrecked their cars, cut themselves, overdosed on drugs or beaten each other senseless. The nurse led us to a room whose other occupant was not a student.

It was Alfred Hastings. He was seated on the edge of the bed, a bandage around his torso, manacled and in leg irons. He glowered at each cop in turn. When my oversized prisoner saw him he said, "What the fuck they do to you, man?"

"The bastards shot me."

"No shit?"

"Yeah. They won't say which one of 'em done it but I'm gonna find out. When I get loose again I'm gonna come back and kill him."

It was a threat he repeated on several occasions. Most cops, including this writer, live with death threats. So do many judges. But Hastings' threat was especially stupid because it allowed the police to checkmate his lawyer's attempt to get him out on ten percent of his bond. Because of his expressed intention to kill a policeman, he was held in jail in lieu of the full half-million dollar bail.

That was not his only act of stupidity. When Teresa Harris, the admissions clerk, asked him his occupation, he replied, "armed robber." She looked at Officer Steve Clark, an eyebrow raised.

"Put it down," Clark said. "If that's what he claims to be, he has a right to say so." So that is what was entered on the admissions form, which was introduced in evidence at his trial. Public Defender Michael Westfall tried to have it thrown out on the ground that Hastings had not at that point been read his rights, but the court ruled against him. Westfall should have known better because the questioner was not a law officer but a hospital admitting clerk; the question was routinely asked of all admittees; it had only to do with background, not criminal activity; Hastings was not under interrogation; and he was under no obligation to identify himself as a professional outlaw anyway.

Clearly, he took a certain pride in his craft and in his professionalism, which was high. But I would call it into question. When I examined his gun I found it rusty in spots, and pitted. It had not been cleaned since the last time it was fired. No true professional treats his gun that carelessly.

A nurse came in and ran the curtain between the two beds, effectively cutting off the conversation between Hastings and my outsized prisoner with the sliced hand.

I went to the front-most edge of the curtain, from where I could keep an eye on my prisoner and examine Hastings' face at the same time. It was a strange face, baleful, like that of a schoolyard bully surrounded by smaller boys determined not to take any more. That was what the drawings did not capture. Even the one done from the description of McAllister did not project Hastings' attitude of resentful belligerence, which is obvious in Illustrations No. 24, 25, and 26. I noted this belligerence when Hastings saw I was studying his face.

"Hey, whatta *you* staring at?"

"You, pal."

"I ain't your pal. Whatta you looking at me for?"

"If I told you," I said, "you wouldn't believe it, so why bother?" I was thinking of the many times I had drawn this face from what other people thought they remembered, and of how far off the target their memories and the resultant drawings were.

Hastings asked my name, and I showed it to him on the metal name tag pinned to my shirt.

"Here," I said, "read it yourself, so you won't forget it."

"A tough guy," he said. "Okay, tough guy, I ever get outta here I'm gonna find out how tough you are."

"I'm terrified," I said. I started to add that he'd do well to begin by getting rid of the roll of fat around his middle, but a doctor came into the room and the subject was changed.

Meanwhile, the big man with the sliced hand refused treatment. The examining physician tried to talk him into some stitches, because it was indeed a bad cut, but had to admit that because no tendons were damaged nor major blood vessels severed, my prisoner would probably get

ILLUSTRATION No.24   Hastings being returned to jail by Corrections Officer Allen Flickinger.

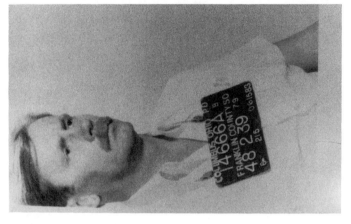

Courtesy of Franklin County, Ohio
Sherriff's Department.

ILLUSTRATION No.25 Mug shot of Alfred Hastings
(front view).

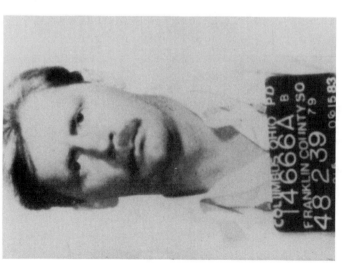

Courtesy of Franklin County, Ohio
Sherriff's Department.

ILLUSTRATION No.26 Mug shot of Alfred Hastings
(three-quarter view). Note the development of
the depressor muscles at the corner of the mouth.

along fine if he could avoid infection. As soon as he was patched up we took him to jail, where he was apprised of his and his assailant's right to file for compensation as victims of crime. Because both had been injured in the fight, under Ohio law both were technically "victims of crime" and therefore eligible to apply for compensation. They went through the motions of filling out the forms, but the maneuver got nowhere, and I understand that that potential for bamboozlement has been plugged up.

As I approached the dispatcher's area I heard the computer begin to grind. Normally this happens in response to a simple request such as a license check or a social security check, and these replies are usually not more than a few lines. This time the machine just kept on cranking, The sheet of paper kept coming, grew longer, passed the edge of the table and snaked toward the floor.

"What in hell is *that*?" I asked.

"That's Hastings' rap sheet."

It was just about four feet long when the machine stopped. Most of the charges were for armed robbery, escape from jail and concealed weapons, and they covered the entire northern quadrant east of the Mississippi to New England.

CHAPTER 9

Trials and Tribulations

In many cases, contrary to popular belief, the guilt or innocence of the accused is not determined in court before judge and jury. It is tested time and again long before any trial, and in many instances the charges are reduced or dropped altogether.

At the street level, the officer will avoid making a weak arrest because he doesn't want to get criticized by his immediate supervisor. For exactly the same reason, the supervisor will not take such an arrest to the prosecutor; and the prosecutor will not take a case to the grand jury if he thinks there is insufficient probable cause. That is where plea bargaining enters the picture.

That is why the guilt or innocence of the accused is constantly tested in the whole judicial process from street arrest to jury trail. This is why Professor H. Richard Uviller of Columbia University Law School asserts that defense attorneys almost never have the luxury of defending someone who is in fact innocent (*Tempered Zeal*, 1988). Once in a while, of course, a truly innocent person will make it all the way through the criminal justice system from street arrest to prison without getting kicked off the line at some inspection point along the way, but he is a relatively rare bird. TV shows like *Matlock* and *Perry Mason* would have us think this happens every Tuesday and Sunday night, but the fact is, it occurs only rarely. There are those in the civil libertarian community who feel it should *never* happen, period. The problem is, the criminal justice system is composed of human beings; and to impose absolutes on any such system is to invite its collapse.

But we try. Probable cause is tested at every level—street arrest, departmental review, prosecutor, grand jury—before a case ever comes to trial. At the trial court level we do everything within reason to stack the deck in favor of the accused. That too is as it should be; the spectre of false imprisonment haunts everyone, police included.

So we insist that the prosecutor establish proof beyond reasonable doubt in the minds of all twelve jurors, whereas the defense has only to cast doubt of such proof in the mind of just one juror. A fair analogy would be a twelve-round prizefight in which the defending champion had only to win one round in order to be declared the victor. Where human freedom is at stake, a simple majority will not do.

Thus, two elements attain paramount importance: jury selection and acting skills.

In Ohio, each side is allowed four "pre-empts," that is, peremptory dismissals from a jury panel on the preference of the attorneys. Prosecutors like to empanel, if possible, factory foremen, retired Army colonels, friends of policemen, farmers and hard-headed businessmen. Defense attorneys prefer librarians, English professors, interior decorators, clergymen, musicians, artists, and people active in liberal causes.

After jury selection come the histrionics. The defense knows that the accused, if he comes to trial at all, has already convinced a lot of perfectly sane folk he is guilty as sin, so he knows that one of his best tools for sowing doubt in the mind of just one juror lies in his ability to create the illusion of innocence where none exists. For this he needs acting skill. Some defense attorneys take acting courses at local community colleges. The author knows one who is an accomplished semiprofessional actor who plays in summer stock to good reviews. If this takes time away from his practice, it certainly sharpens his courtroom skills. The result of such efforts is that American courtroom trials are often good theater rather than good legal practice.

However, justice and the illusion of justice are frequently opposites. If the adversarial nature of our legal system insists that justice, from the perspective of the defense, is only served by acquittal of the accused, regardless of guilt or innocence, then it follows that the defense may employ illusions that convey the precise opposite of the truth. One such set of illusions has to do with the physical appearance of the defendent; good theatre is often aided by good stage props.

In other words, there are ways to commit perjury without actually telling lies in court, and a good defense attorney knows them all. Because ethics and morality are not amenable to precise measurement, it is difficult if not impossible to say when ordinary prudence shades off into calculated deception. However, a couple of examples might help. For instance, a lawyer who allows a pimp charged with organized prostitution to show up in court attired in a flashy suit, silk shirt and pink flowered necktie is not only stupid, he is negligent as a lawyer. But if that same lawyer were to dress a successful politician in dirty overalls to project a populist image for the purpose of fooling a jury, he would be guilty of humbuggery. The client, who has taken an oath to tell the truth, is in fact (if not in spoken word) telling a lie about his identity; and his attorney, who has taken no such oath, is an accessory to the deception.

This is what D.F. Pace and J.C. Styles mean when they say, "the moral and legal question as to where legal advice stops and criminal conspiracy begins is critical to the control of . . . crime. (*Organized Crime: Concepts and Control*, Prentice-Hall 1975, p. 36.)

Any police investigator, including any police artist, runs into this problem very early on.

A few years ago a fellow named Dickerson, who lived in a trailer in Nelsonville, Ohio, was charged with the shotgun murder of a friend who, along with a female companion, happened to be in the trailer with Dickerson. He was also charged with transporting the victim to a remote rural area and shooting him a second time to make sure he was dead—all in the presence of the female companion, a nurse. The principals' accounts of what actually happened, and the various defense alibis offered and repeatedly altered, are so convoluted as to defy any final solution, and at this point they don't matter anyway. What is significant is that Mr. Dickerson, who could not afford an attorney, was assigned to the Public Defender, one Michael Westfall.

Among other things Dickerson could not afford was decent attire. Mr. Westfall corrected this theatrical shortcoming by marching Mr. Dickerson down to a local haberdashery, where he outfitted the defendant in a conservative three-piece business suit costing three hundred dollars and charged it to the taxpayers of Athens County. Westfall also extended the public largesse to include a clean new shirt and necktie. It is not recorded whether Westfall taught his client how to knot it.

In any case, Dickerson showed up in court looking uncomfortable and ill at ease in his new Sunday-go-to-meeting duds, which looked about as appropriate on him as a prayer shawl on Al Capone.

A number of people, including the author, were more disgusted than amused by this grotesquerie. In a guest editorial of the day I wrote, in part,

> "...the notion—naive perhaps—held by many of us is that the object of criminal justice ought to be precisely that: justice. By which we mean neither convicting the innocent nor turning loose the human jackals among us without regard to the consequences. We mean instead a serious inquiry into the truth, an inquiry divested of the legalistic maneuvering, the loophole seeking, the juggling acts, the bombast, the histrionics, the precedence given to form over substance and the striving after illusions that have cast discredit on recent local trials...
>
> "At the heart of such disregard is an acceptance of artifice as a legitimate device. The purchase of expensive clothing for indigent defendants from public funds is a good example. The object of such disbursements—notwithstanding the pious protests of defense counsel—is to create the illusion of something that is not true. I think any fair-minded person would agree a defendent ought to be permitted to present himself clean and neatly attired in the clothes he normally wears to appear well before his friends. But to present a man to his peers

attired in clothing that is far beyond his means and totally out of character is an insult to the intelligence of the jury. To do so at public expense is inexcusable. It has the effect of telling a lie, and in that sense it is a cynical device for circumventing the oath to tell the truth, the whole truth and nothing but the truth."

This entry on the editorial page did not deter Westfall from the same tactic in the trial of John Salyers, but it did at least cause him to shift the expense of Salyers' unwonted sartorial splendor from the public coffers to the family of the accused. Illustration No. 27 demonstrates the marvels of illusion defense attorneys can create. On the left is John Salyers, knife fighter and murderer, at the time of his arrest. On the right is the magically transformed John Salyers, resplendent in his new finery; he could be on his way to preach the gospel were he not at that moment on trial for his life.

Verbal reports of action in progress are often as inexact as physical descriptions given to police artists. In Chapter 1 we noted that a youth named Ricky Martello saw Steve Kempton punch the victim and concluded that it was Kempton not Salyers who did the stabbing. This was at variance with the testimony of other witnesses and with an interview the police had with one Maxine Lowry, who overheard a conversation between Kempton and Salyers. But it was extremely important to Westfall; if he could use Martello's testimony to raise a reasonable doubt in the mind of just one juror, he could possibly get a hung jury. Westfall's assertion in court that it was Kempton who killed Mendelson was based on the following portion of the taped transcript of Martello's interview with the police:

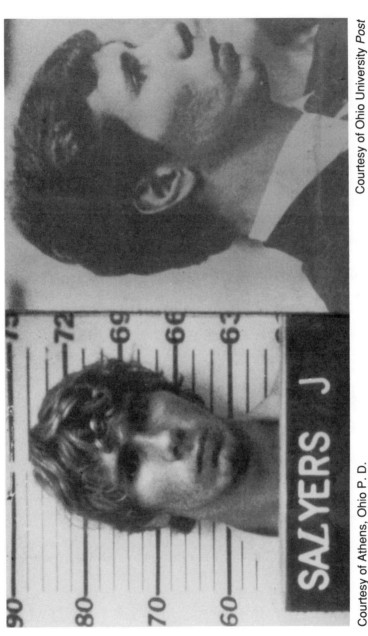

Courtesy of Athens, Ohio P. D.

Courtesy of Ohio University *Post*

ILLUSTRATION No.27 Defense lawyer miracles. At left, John Salyers immediately after knife murder of Mendelson. At right, Salyers in conservative business suit at time of trial.

Lt. Cogar: Tell me about it, will you?

Martello: What I saw. . .I heard, well from what I saw, all I saw was he got cut and when he was running away, I thought maybe, you know, some people that get cut, er, you know jarred or something, get scared and start running around, you know, and might get to his car, he might have bled to death so I told two of my friends we better follow him and see if he's all right. . . .

Lt. Cogar: Tell me, who stabbed him?

Martello: I know, I only know, I think his name's Steve Kempton, I'm not sure about his last name, but I know his first name.

Lt. Cogar: Tell me about how he, how, tell me the way it happened down there, okay? Stand right here where I can look at you.

Martello: Well. . . .

Lt. Cogar: You saw him get stabbed, right?

Martello: Yeah, this is how I saw. . . .

Lt. Cogar: Well then, tell me that, tell me about that, what happened? They were arguing or what?

Martello: See we were just coming from the, from down I don't know, down this way, and when I, when I came, I saw 'em fighting, and all of a sudden (Mendelsohn) grabbed his neck.

Lt. Cogar: Okay. You were coming from where? Court Street? Or coming from Dexter's, which direction?

Martello: Yeh, Dexter's, Dexter's.

Immediately after the stabbing, however, Kempton and Salyers had gone to the apartment of Carlos and Maxine Lowry. At the Lowry place they conversed briefly and then fell asleep sitting up in chairs. It was during this conversation, overheard by Maxine Lowry, that Salyers told Kempton he was pretty sure he had

killed Mendelson and invited Kempton to go back uptown and "watch me kill a nigger." The police taped the
interview with Maxine Lowry, recorded here in part:

Capt. Beasley: The time is now 7:12 and present is Mrs.
Carlos Lowry. Mrs. Lowry, I need for you to tell me
what, uh, what you overheard the night when Steve
Kempton and John Salyers, Jr., came into your apartment
here.

Lowry: Well, I was in bed, but I was awake, and I
couldn't tell you exactly what time it was, but it was late
and I heard John say, "man I've got human blood all over
me, I'm scared," and uh, he said, "I think I killed that guy,
Steve." And Steve didn't say much of anything, and then
he said, uh, "ya wanna go back uptown with me, Steve,
you wanna see me kill a nigger?" Steve didn't wanna go,
so they didn't go, but John said that, let's see, he stuck a
knife in that guy then he ripped it. And that was all I
heard.

Capt. Beasley: Okay.

It was at the Lowry place that the two were arrested.
The police had gone to the home of Kempton's girlfriend,
who told them he was currently staying with a friend
called Snook. Lt. Cogar recognized this as the alias of
Carlos Lowry, who lived just two blocks down the street
from the modest house where Salyers lived with his
grandmother.

Under Ohio law all of the foregoing is discoverable.
There is a point in the pretrial process called Discovery,
which operates like a poker hand when the bets are
called. That is, both prosecution and defense are required
by law to lay all pertinent evidence on the table. Either
side may thus object to the subsequent admission of un-

declared evidence and have it ruled inadmissable. Defense attorneys are especially sensitive to this protective device against unfair surprises. That is one of the many reasons Professor Uviller said that defense attorneys seldom get to defend people they know to be innocent.

But the problem of getting a conviction on Salyers did not center on his identification as the one who actually did the stabbing. The number of witnesses, together with Ricky Martello's own uncertainty, made it easy to knock down Westfall's attempt to throw suspicion on Kempton. The big problems had to do with the precise charge and with one of the twelve jurors.

There are three elements necessary for a charge of aggravated murder (in some states called first-degree or premeditated murder): (1) purposely (2) with prior calculation or design (3) cause another's death. The key element, and the one that distinguishes aggravated murder from simple murder, is the second: "with prior calculation or design." The amount of time necessary to justify that element is a matter of interpretation. Admittedly, Salyers didn't have long to contemplate the act. A witness named Joe Wells stated that he saw Salyers fingering the knife behind his back briefly—perhaps a few seconds—before swinging it at the victim. The prosecutor, Michael Ward, conferred with his staff and decided that given Salyers' reputation as a knife fighter, a few seconds were sufficient for him to contemplate and go for the kill. Ward opted for the aggravated murder charge with death specification as distinct from simple murder, which lacks the element of premeditation and carries in Ohio only fifteen years to life.

The other problem surfaced in jury selection. Both sides had exhausted their four "preempts," with one juror remaining to be chosen. The prosecution thought it had things in the bag because the next qualified juror in line was the wife of a state trooper. At that point, however, the trooper's wife turned to a young woman seated next to her and, referring to Salyers, remarked, "I wonder how much it cost to dress that scumbag up in a suit like that?"

The young woman to whom she made the remark was a college student named Maria Malatesta (pseudonym), and she was outraged. Quickly scribbling a note, she passed it to the judge. The latter, after verifying that the trooper's wife had indeed made the comment, dismissed her for cause and replaced her with the next qualified person, who happened to be Ms. Malatesta herself.

"Occupation?"

"Church organist."

The prosecuting team rolled their eyes. Two categories at one stroke: a musician *and* a churchy type. There goes the whole ball game, they thought. It almost turned out that way.

Malatesta, it seems, was not just a church organist. She was also a college student, which added a third dimension to her value for the defense; and, to nail down a fourth, she was a music therapy major. The prosecutorial team agreed that there wasn't much chance of getting a conviction past such an array of pro-defense prejudices. College students are traditionally sympathetic to the accused, whom they generally perceive to be the underdogs; and students in the helping professions, especially those preparing for therapy work of any kind, are uncommonly vulnerable to tales of misfortune.

The forebodings of the prosecution were well-founded. The first jury poll, taken after only twenty minutes, came out eleven to one for conviction on aggravated murder. Malatesta, predictably, had voted for acquittal. During the discussion that followed she told the other members of the jury that if they would reduce the charge to simple murder (one of the options legally available to Ohio jurors), thus eliminating the possibility of a death sentence, she would go along with it.

A second poll, taken on the simple murder charge, just as predictably came up eleven to one; Malatesta had once again voted for acquittal. She next expressed the belief that manslaughter would be more appropriate. She argued that since Mendelson presented such a formidable aspect, Salyers had no doubt acted in self-defense. Besides, the poor boy had had such an unfortunate childhood.

At that point the forewoman of the jury slammed her fist down and said, in effect, *no-goddammit-no!* You made a deal and you are going to keep the faith with us. I am *not* going down to manslaughter, and I am *not* going to report a hung jury. We are *not* going home early. We are going to stay here in this room for the next year, if necessary, until we get the vote you agreed on."

It took eleven of them six more hours to wear Malatesta down, but the jury finally emerged with a unanimous vote on the murder charge. Malatesta was crying openly as Salyers was given fifteen years to life.

She made an immediate appointment to visit him at the county jail that very day, at 2:00 P.M.. Michael Ward and his two assistant prosecutors, probably anticipating a conspiracy to commit an escape from custody, wisely arranged to have him transferred to prison before the meeting could take place. Nevertheless it is reported that Malatesta did later visit him in prison, guitar at the ready, to undertake his rehabilitation via the music therapy route.

It is unknown to this writer how long she kept it up. In any case, John Salyers may be the only felon in the history of American penology to receive free guitar lessons from a juror whose vote was necessary to send him to prison in the first place.

"Do you think she fell in love with Salyers?" I asked Assistant Prosecutor Dave Warren, on a recent trip to Athens.

"Oh, unquestionably. It was written all over her. She couldn't take her eyes off him."

It was about then that I got a call from one of our resident FBI agents about a small-time hoodlum named Perry Bennett; who had escaped from the penitentiary in Chillicothe and was thought to have crossed state lines. He was also thought to have changed his appearance. Could I do a couple of sketches to anticipate what he might look like?

I did not know this assignment was to get me involved in the whole subject of terrorist disguises and lead to new fields of interest.

CHAPTER 10

Terrorism and Terrorist Disguises

Special Agent Todd Hanson, FBI, is what anyone would call a good cop. A former New Jersey state trooper, he brings to his job a treasury of street smarts and a physique like that of a fully-conditioned linebacker. More important, he has avoided the magisterial insularity often attributed, fairly or unfairly, to some members of federal investigative agencies. His dedication is to the whole corpus of law enforcement. He is the kind of guy you like to have on your side, and when he was transferred to Washington we were all sorry to see him go.

Once when Todd learned I was planning to do surveillance on suspected drug activity in a rural area, he volunteered to meet me at 4:00 A.M. "It's too dangerous out there alone," he said. "You might need backup."

So when he phoned me about Perry Bennett I dropped what I was doing and went to his office. I figured I owed him one.

Bennett had escaped from Chillicothe where he was serving time for burglary, and was rumored to have headed South, probably to Alabama or Georgia. This raised the charge of unlawful flight to avoid confinement, a federal offense the moment the escapee crosses state lines. Information sources also reported he had grown a beard.

Hanson gave me two mug shots of Bennett, one front-face and the other a profile. Exact copies of these shots appear in Illustration No. 28. What would Bennett look like with facial hair?

The first thing you notice about his face, especially in profile, is that he has a grossly undershot jaw; it protrudes like the blade on a snow plow. This protrusion actually begins with the lower lip, so that the space between the upper lip and the base of the nose is sharply recessed, forming a notch in the otherwise relatively even progression from chin to forehead. In profile this distortion would still be observable with a beard, or even with a combination of beard and mustache (see Illustration No. 29).

However, if Bennett were shrewd enough to grow only a bushy mustache he would fill in the recessed space between his nose and mouth. This would be his best disguise because it would straighten out the line of his profile (see Illustration No. 30).

By this time I had become interested in seeing how Bennett might alter his appearance in other ways. I did a series of drawings from the original mug shots showing him in various combinations of hair styles, with facial hair and eyeglasses, both from the front and in profile. They are not pertinent here, but they served to underscore something I hadn't thought much about before: there is a world of difference between a *disguise* and a mere *distractor*. A disguise is what you wear to make you look like something you are not. It can be complicated, expensive, uncomfortable and a bloody nuisance. It can be some-

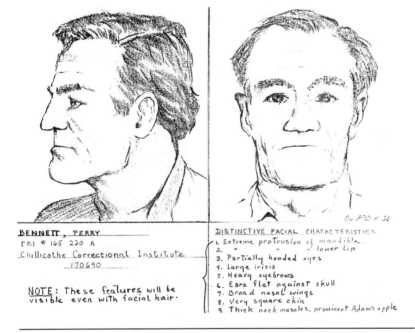

BENNETT, PERRY
FBI # 165 220 A
Chillicothe Correctional Institute
170690

NOTE: These features will be visible even with facial hair.

DISTINCTIVE FACIAL CHARACTERISTICS
1. Extreme protrusion of mandible.
2. " " " lower lip
3. Partially hooded eyes
4. Large irisis
5. Heavy eyebrows
6. Ears flat against skull
7. Broad nasal wings
8. Very square chin
9. Thick neck muscles, prominent Adam's apple

ILLUSTRATION No. 28 From an FBI mug shot of Perry Bennett (with thanks to special agent Todd Hanson). Note extreme undershot jaw.

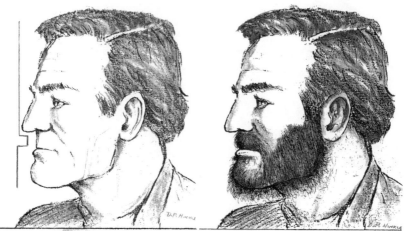

BENNETT, PERRY
FBI # 165 220 A
Chillicothe Correctional Institute
170690

ILLUSTRATION No. 29 Perry Bennett in profile. Note that postulated beard and mustache do not help to disguise him.

ILLUSTRATION No. 30 Perry Bennett with mustache only. Note how it fills the irregular notch in his profile. This would be his best disguise.

thing as simple as a ski mask or as complicated as the complete attire of the opposite sex. It can be subtle or clumsy. A couple of years ago in Canton, Ohio, a bank teller looked up to see a large black robber dressed in a skirt and a woman's wig. He had even gone to the trouble of donning a D-cup brassiere stuffed with two large grapefruit. He had neglected, however, to cover his blacksmith arms and he made no attempt to disguise his basso profundo voice. It was clear, too, that he wasn't accustomed to walking in high heels. His robbery career was short lived. Ludicrous as his outfit was, it serves as a good example of a disguise.

A distractor, however, is something that merely draws the viewer's attention away from what you don't want him to notice. The best example I can think of was provided by a bank robber who wore a simple orange Band-Aid® on one cheek. Every teller in the bank remembered the Band-Aid®, but none could give a description of the face it was stuck to. It was found on the sidewalk outside the bank, thrown there as the robber sprinted down the street.

As I worked on the Perry Bennett drawings, it occurred to me that people who are trying to live unobserved or incognito don't go around in disguise, nor do they wear ski masks except for the few seconds when they are actively engaged in a robbery, kidnapping or act of terrorism. They use distractors.

The rest of the time terrorists have to resort to less dramatic means of hiding their identity. The kidnappers of Patty Hearst lived for a long time in a Pennsylvania farmhouse, coming and going dressed in the garb of local country folk, and they left the area without ever being identified. The Manning gang was likewise able to escape the notice of lawmen for a long time before being captured in Ohio. Manning himself, with his wife, made it to Virginia where he lived a low profile life for months before being apprehended. Marilyn Buck was arrested near Dobbs Ferry, New York, almost within rifle shot of the scene of the Brinks holdup for which she had driven the getaway car four years earlier. All of these people were following the counsel of the late Brazilian theoretician, Carlos Marighella, in his pamphlet, *Minimanual of the Urban Guerrilla*:: "The urban guerrilla," he states, "must know how to live among the people and must be careful not to appear strange. . . .He must not wear clothes that are different from those that other people wear."

That is fine as long as the terrorist is unknown to authorities; but once identity is determined and mug shots or police sketches become available, the underground terrorist or "urban guerrilla" has the double task of living an apparently normal life and making sure outward appearances differ from those of published photos or sketches.

That is where distractors come in. For the most part they fall into four categories:

— **eyeglasses**
— **clothing**
— **hair**
— **cosmetics**

Let's see how each of these is applied by terrorists to deflect our view from the features most likely to give them away. By improving our ability to recognize known dangerous persons we reduce the threat they pose at all levels—national, local, personal. In order to do this, we must beat the terrorist at his own game. That is not easy, because many terrorists are highly skilled in the use of distractors.

Marilyn Jean Buck is a case in point. Reportedly the only white member of the Black Liberation Army, she drove the getaway car in the 1981 Brinks armored car robbery at Nyack, New York, during which two police officers were killed. In the course of the incident she managed to shoot herself in the leg, which resulted in a permanent limp. In spite of this, she succeeded in avoiding arrest for four years.

She was able to do so because she is a master of diguise. Of the eight photographs of this woman I have examined, no two appear to be of the same individual. She seems able on short notice to project a wide variety of personalities: pretty secretary, scrubwoman, housewife, gun moll, hippie and others. In each photo her hair is markedly different, and she sports an interesting assortment of eyeglasses.

Careful examination of her face, however, reveals two related facts: first, it has a number of irregularities and imbalances she could not hide short of major plastic surgery and which can be easily seen by anyone who knows what to look for; and second, she knows how to cover most of them up.

She is not dumb, this Marilyn Buck. She has obviously analyzed her own face very carefully and has noted, among other things, that her eyes are extraordinarily far apart. In like manner, her cheekbones are very wide like those of certain Siberian racial stocks, giving her whole face a sort of flat appearance. It happens she also has very poor eyesight and must wear prescription lenses. Furthermore, one iris is darker than the other.

When she chooses frames for her lenses, does she go

for those that fit her face? Hardly. In every instance her glasses are either far too large or far too small. The too-large frames tend to obliterate both the flatness of her face and the distance between the eyes, whereas the too-small frames tend to cause the eyes to appear closer together (see Illustrations No. 31 and 32).

Those are not her only features that are out of kilter. Her nose appears to have collided with a fast-moving hard object, such as a fist, leaving it out of line, with one nostril noticeably smaller than the other. Her mouth is clearly out of balance; both the upper and lower lips are thicker and heavier on the right side of her face. Her chin angles forward like a chisel or the blade of a block plane.

But the imbalance that most arrests our attention, and which is obviously beyond plastic surgery, involves the two halves of her face. Notice in Illustration No. 33 that the vertical and horizontal axes do not form 90 degree angles. Instead, they intersect to form two sets of adjacent angles of approximately 85 degrees and 95 degrees—a distortion clear enough to be observed by almost anybody. Her face is clearly heavier and lower on the right side.

Some of these features can be neutralized with distractors, but others cannot. The eyes and cheekbones are relatively easy to distort by the careful selection of glasses and the mouth is susceptible to illusion with the skillful application of lipstick. The nose, however, can be corrected only with surgery, which is both expensive and likely to invite unwelcome attention.

The chin involves basic bone structure and, like the nose, can't be easily disguised. And the basic imbalance of the two halves of her face is a giveaway totally beyond the reach of ordinary cosmetics.

CHEEK BONES
VERY WIDE AND
FLAT

EYES SET
WIDE

NOSE APPEARS
BROKEN

MOUTH OUT
OF BALANCE

CHISEL CHIN

VERTICAL AND
HORIZONTAL AXES DO
NOT FORM 90° ANGLES

D. P. HINKLE

ILLUSTRATION No. 31 Marilyn Jean Buck, now in prison. Note the features that can't be disguised. Sketches made from FBI wanted posters.

MARILYN JEAN BUCK

FBI No. 618 192 H
ESCAPED FEDERAL PRISONER;
CONSPIRACY TO COMMIT ARMED BANK ROBBERY
F.P.C.:   21 M 9 U 000 20

L 2 U 00I

DESCRIPTION

AGE: 35, born December 13, 1947, Temple, Texas
HEIGHT: 5'8''   EYES: brown
WEIGHT: 130 pounds   COMPLEXION: fair
BUILD: medium   RACE: white
HAIR: brown (known to wear wigs and scarves)   NATIONALITY: American
OCCUPATIONS: laboratory technologist, librarian, photographer, printer, secretary,
                       typesetter, clerk
SCARS AND MARKS: scar on left arm; scar on right leg below the knee from gunshot
                             wound
REMARKS: must wear prescription glasses or contact lenses; left eye heavily
pigmented, having blue and brown colors; known to have allergies; takes medication
for thyroid condition; health food user; reportedly knowledgeable in Spanish
language.
SOCIAL SECURITY NUMBERS USED: 068-44-5380; 271-68-7809; 332-78-4553;
333-68-7214; 358-64-5266; 360-44-2424; 452-73-2635; 453-84-3652;
454-72-5136; 546-06-5917; 547-11-3383; 556-70-0938; 952-64-4256;
953-47-6721; 556-70-0930; 068-44-5380

ILLUSTRATION No. 32 Marilyn Jean Buck. Various mug shots from FBI
wanted posters.

MARILYN JEAN BUCK

FBI No 618 192 H
ESCAPED FEDERAL PRISONER
  CONSPIRACY TO COMMIT
  ARMED BANK ROBBERY
F P C   21 M 9 U 000 20
            L 2 U 00I
Retouched photograph taken 1974
  Date retouched photographs taken unknown

DESCRIPTION

AGE 34 born December 13 1947 Temple Texas
HEIGHT 5'8"   Eyes brown
WEIGHT 130 pounds   COMPLEXION fair
BUILD medium   RACE white
HAIR brown (known to wear wigs and scarves) NATIONALITY American
OCCUPATIONS laboratory technologist, librarian photographer printer
                     secretary typesetter clerk
SCARS AND MARKS scar on left arm
REMARKS must wear prescription glasses or contact lenses left eye is
heavily pigmented having blue and brown colors known to have allergies
takes medication for thyroid condition health food user reportedly
knowledgeable in Spanish language
SOCIAL SECURITY NUMBERS USED 271-68 7809 332-78-4563
333-68 7214 358-64-5266 360-44 2424 452-73-2635 453-84 3852
454-72-5136 546-06-5917 547-11-3383 556-70 0938 952-64 4256
953-47-6721 556-70-0930 088-44-5380

ILLUSTRATION NO. 33   Analysis of Buck's face. Note vertical and horizontal lines do not form right angles.

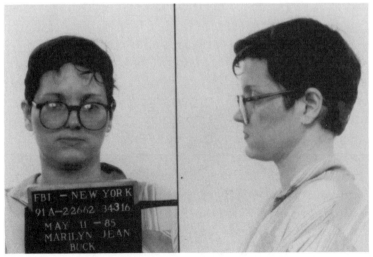

ILLUSTRATION NO. 34 Recent mug shots of Marilyn Jean Buck following her arrest at Dobbs Ferry, N.Y. Note that weight gain has not changed basic features. Note also large eyeglasses.

But most faces have too many areas of imbalance to make it practical to cover them all (see Illustration No. 34).

For example, Joanne Chesimard's face is a mass of ir-regularities. Like Marilyn Buck, she is said to be a master of disguise. The number of personalities she assumes is testimony to that assertion, and may be one reason why she has been at large since 1979 after escaping from Attica (New York) State Prison, where she was serving a life sentence for the murder of a policeman in a terrorist incident. She has reportedly since been seen in Cuba, but this lacks vertification.

Various photos of Chesimard depict a trim business-woman, a bespectacled librarian, a housewife and a flirt. In two of the photos she wears conservative clothing, in another a checked shirt, in still another a print blouse. In one of the snapshots she wears glasses with enormous frames. The inexperienced observer could be pardoned for assuming that these photos are four different women.

Let's examine her features in Illustration No. 35. The most telling anomaly in Joanne Chesimard's face is that one eye—her left—is heavily hooded, whereas the other is not. If you read lots of spy stories by people such as Ian Fleming or John LeCarré you may assert that this can be corrected by plastic surgery; but common sense suggests the expense would be prohibitive for most terrorists. In any case, it would leave several other areas of imbalance.

For example, her jaw line on the left side bows inward to form an S-curve, whereas her right jawline forms a perfectly normal arc. Moreover, her upper lip is slightly longer from side to side than the lower lip—somewhat unusual in blacks of West, Central or South African origin.

JOANNE DEBORAH CHESIMARD

FBI No. 11 102 J7
INTERSTATE FLIGHT, MURDER
F.P.C.: 7 1 aAa 11
          1 aAa
Photographs taken 1979, 1980; date unknown

DESCRIPTION

AGE 35 born July 16, 1947, New York, New York
           (not supported by birth record)
HEIGHT: 5'6"   EYES: brown
WEIGHT: 127 to 138 pounds   COMPLEXION: medium
BUILD: slender   RACE: Negro
HAIR: black (various styles)   NATIONALITY: American
SCARS AND MARKS: bullet scars on abdomen, chest, left shoulder and under
                          side of right arm; round scar on left knee
OCCUPATIONS: tutor, writer
REMARKS Has worn tinted prescription glasses in the past; may be dressed
              in Muslim or men's clothing; reportedly jogs regularly
SOCIAL SECURITY NUMBER USED: 051 38 5131

JOANNE DEBORAH CHESIMARD **DESCRIPTION**

FBI No. 11 102 J7
INTERSTATE FLIGHT - MURDER
F.P.C.: 7 1 aAa 11
          1 aAa
Photographs taken 1979

AGE: 32, born July 16, 1947, New York, New York (not supported by
           birth records)
HEIGHT: 5'6"   EYES: maroon
WEIGHT: 127 to 138 pounds   COMPLEXION: medium
BUILD: slender   RACE: Negro
HAIR: black   NATIONALITY: American
SCARS AND MARKS: bullet scars on abdomen, chest, left shoulder and
                          underside of right arm; round scar on left knee
OCCUPATIONS: tutor, writer
REMARKS: May be wearing Afro hair style.
SOCIAL SECURITY NUMBER USED: 051-38-5131

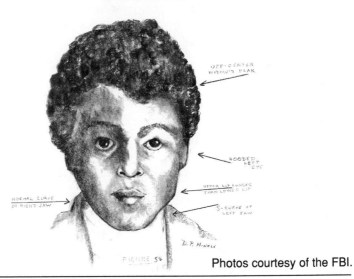

Photos courtesy of the FBI.

ILLUSTRATION No. 35   Joanne Chesimard.   Above: FBI mug shots.
Below: facial analysis.   Note imbalances.

But the feature that grabs our attention most quickly is her forehead: it is completely out of balance. This is the part most easily covered by hair or headgear, but for some reason she hasn't bothered to cover it. She has a pronounced widow's peak to the left of center, leaving a very high recession on the right side as compared to the left.

There is nothing Joanne Chesimard can do to hide her face from the sharp observer. She may be regarded as a master of disguise, but in fact she is only clever at distracting attention.

Richard Scutari, on the other hand, doesn't have to worry about jawlines or mouth shapes. His fast-growing black beard allows him to change facial hair combinations with relative ease. A right wing extremist, Scutari has had a diversified career as tavern owner, martial arts instructor, diver and construction worker. He is charged with a wide variety of federal offenses and is thought to be involved in the stockpiling of firearms and ammunition, presumably for the use of right wing terrorists.

Although various FBI photos of Scutari show him in a number of different beard and hair styles, several anomalies are obvious: a long down-pointed nose with a large round tip; eyelids that slant upward as they approach the nasal bridge; a high forehead that recedes more on the right than on the left; heavy, thick eyebrows; and a very short distance between nose and mouth (see Illustration No. 36).

Even though a person may appear to have a fairly "average" face, it is likely to exhibit a whole range of irregularities; no matter what people do to disguise such irregularities, they can't cover them all. The best they can do is to pick the best shot and pray for luck. If they have

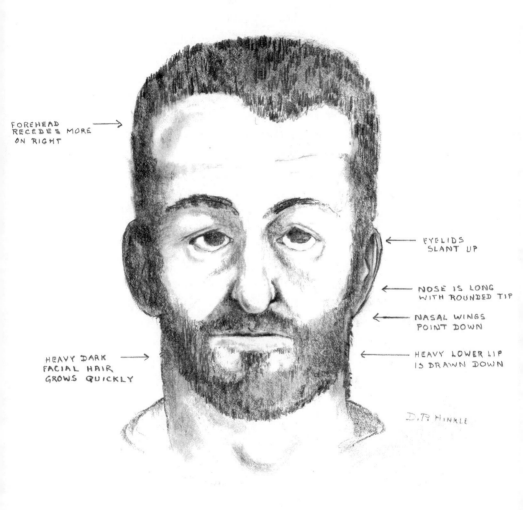

FOREHEAD
RECEDES MORE
ON RIGHT

EYELIDS
SLANT UP

NOSE IS LONG
WITH ROUNDED TIP

NASAL WINGS
POINT DOWN

HEAVY DARK
FACIAL HAIR
GROWS QUICKLY

HEAVY LOWER LIP
IS DRAWN DOWN

D.R. HINKLE

ILLUSTRATION No. 36 John Scutari. Facial analysis based on FBI
wanted poster.

brains enough to analyze their own faces, they can usually pick one or two characteristics that, if disguised or obliterated, can lead investigators astray.

From time to time we hear of a terrorist or bank bandit using a stocking mask. We read of witnesses who give fairly good descriptions of physiques, clothing, voice and direction of flight, but who say, "I can't describe his face because he was wearing a stocking mask."

Let's examine this. A stocking mask (nothing but a cutoff section of a woman's long silk, rayon or nylon hose) has the apparent advantage of allowing you to see through it, but unless it is seen flush against the skin, the fibers throw slight shadows. When it is drawn over the head it permits the wearer to see everything fairly clearly but distorts his image in the eyes of those looking at him.

But a stocking mask distorts that image only in those areas where it is far enough away from contact with the skin to throw a shadow—over the eyes, the base of the nose and the ears (see Illustration No. 37).

A stocking mask really doesn't hide much. It merely clouds the view of the eyes and flattens the tip of the nose. It does absolutely nothing to alter the impression of basic bone structure. For this reason an observant witness can produce a fairly accurate description even if the offender is wearing such as mask (see Illustration No. 38).

You see what you expect to see. The chances are, if you see a face enclosed in a stocking mask you expect to see nothing, and that is what you report. Children draw what they know, not what they see, and that is why they regularly depict houses with at least three sides showing. (It is only much later, when they have outgrown childhood, that they start showing only the two sides actually visible from any one angle.) Adults continue to make the

ILLUSTRATION No. 37 Left: mug shot Robert Bunner. Right: Bunner in stocking mask; photo taken by bank camera.

ILLUSTRATION No. 38 Anonymous robber of convenience store. Note that stocking masks do not rule out good descriptions if you know what to look for.

same mistake: they report what they expect to see, based on what they know.

Thus when they see someone in the attire of a woman, they report seeing "a woman" without really taking a close look. In this age of changing sexual standards it is becoming less unusual to encounter men dressed as women and vice versa. Gay bars abound, and they are patronized by many people who are extremely clever at disguising their sex. Any police officer who has responded to a call to a gay bar has almost certainly been fooled at least once.

This may appear merely inconsequential to some, annoying to others, or even amusing to still others. For terrorism, however, the implications are enormous. We have already noted an incident involving a bank robber who dressed as a woman. Such tactics are becoming increasingly common and increasingly sophisticated.

Whether we are talking about such exotic things as transvestism or merely the distractors employed by a Buck or a Chesimard, or even the hurried make-do efforts of a professional hit man, the principle is very simple. The success of terrorism depends on surprise—an act of violence for which there is no warning. By making recognition of terrorists more likely—or conversely, by reducing the terrorists' chances of escaping early recognition—society gives itself a little time to prepare, prevent, protect.

An offshoot of terrorism is the sense of fear, of foreboding, that pervades a society whose members know that terrorists live among them, faceless and unidentified, and may strike at any time without warning. This is demoralizing and therefore serves one of the terrorist's basic goals: destabilizing the target society. A community's knowledge that terrorists can be recognized in spite of the most elaborate efforts to disguise their faces is potentially one of the best tools for defusing their threat and restoring a measure of public confidence.

By examining in detail the faces of several people who are especially good at using distractors, we have seen they really can't fool us if we know what to look for. For example, a sharp-sighted police officer in Cherry Hill, New Jersey, noted that a suspicious person was wearing spectacles with plain glass for lenses. That may have saved his life; the woman was Lisa Rosenberg, one of the most dangerous American terrorists. She was armed with a machine pistol, fully loaded, and was prepared to kill him if he had given her the chance.

The problem with the term terrorism is that we use it in an unjustifiably restricted sense. When we hear the word we tend to associate it with spectacular acts of violence aimed at influencing political situations, usually at the international level. But in a broader sense, terrorism occurs any time any individual or group of individuals is put in fear by the threat of violence, real or imagined, for any reason—political, social, economic, religious or personal. Any crime against either persons or property falls within this definition of terrorism if it inspires fear or apprehension. To the extent that such fear influences the behavior of people, it succeeds. Spectacular examples such as the Provisional Irish Republican Army (PIRA, or Provos) bombings abound; but even such a low-intensity act as spray-painting graffiti can be classified as terrorism if it influences elderly folk to stay indoors for fear of youth gangs, or influences potential investors to pay less for real estate in areas where such spraying is common.

Most terrorist acts fall somewhere between these extremes. Any eruption of crime, especially if it follows a pattern, gives rise to apprehension ranging from mild alarm to outright terror, depending on the circumstances. We have all seen it happen: a series of rapes will cause people to keep their daughters inside at night, just as a series of burglaries will influence people to lock their doors and windows.

Once in a while you get a one-man crime wave, which is terrorism pure and simple regardless of the intent. Mike White, who ended up getting shot in a gun battle with police, was just such a person. I had a chance to draw his face from several different descriptions.

CHAPTER 11

One Man Crime Wave

In Chapter 9 we noted some of the ways in which the rights of the accused are protected in our legal system, beginning with a presumption of innocence and progressing through a series of stages—reasonable suspicion, probable cause, beyond reasonable doubt—each with increasingly rigid standards of proof.

One consequence of that basic law is that serial criminals, or one-man crime waves, are sometimes not tried for or convicted of multiple offenses—unless the offenses are committed simultaneously or are inextricably tied into the same network of proof. For example, an armed robber who pistol-whips his victim may be convicted at the same time of robbery, felonious assault, and the use of a firearm in the commission of a felony. But that same person may be a solid suspect in a couple dozen robberies and yet be tried for only one of them. Technically, he is innocent of the others until proven guilty. What is significant for society is that a particular series of robberies comes to a screeching halt with the felon's arrest and conviction for any one of them. When he finishes serving his time he may then face trial on the next charge. Meanwhile, though the culprit has not actually been convicted of the other charges, common sense often combines with reason, partial evidence and experience to suggest that if you've solved one you've solved 'em all. That is one of the ways in which crimes sometimes get "cleared" without technically being solved.

Admittedly, the system is awkward, time-consuming, expensive, and at times downright inefficient, but it is a safeguard for which we can all be grateful. It prevents some people properly convicted on one charge from having other convictions added on the basis of mere probable cause or even of suspicion alone. One such person was Michael White, who, though a suspect in many offenses spanning a ten-year period, was convicted of only one—in Athens, anyway.

Mike White was a student at Ohio University in 1973, when he learned the layout of Athens and of Columbus, where his presence is well documented off and on until 1983, and where he was a suspect in a number of rapes. His presence was also well documented in the Portsmouth-Gallipolis area, where he came from originally. Though there were a number of unsolved rapes and minor robberies during the decade 1973-1983 in Athens, I was unaware of his existence until after I began my service with the Athens P. D. Then, early in the spring of '83 began a series of occurrences that produced remarkably similar descriptions of the offender.

There was, for example, a rape on 4 April. The victim was an eighteen-year-old college student who decided to take her dog for a walk at about midnight—in an alley, mind you, behind a string of businesses closed for the night. The dog was not large enough to have protected her against a rabbit, let alone against the medium-sized black male who emerged from the shadow of some bushes.

He was carrying a handgun—a somewhat unusual weapon in rape cases—which he fired once in the general direction of the dog. He ordered the girl into the blackness of a back yard and raped her, then disappeared.

I was called to the P. D. about 2:30 A.M., after the victim had been checked out by the hospital and released. She was a small girl with nondescript features. Her straight shoulder length hair was a lusterless neutral blond, her personality bland. Still badly shaken, she was unable to give much of a description beyond the basics: black male in his late twenties or perhaps early thirties, average build, dark skin, medium height, toboggan cap. Not much to go on, really. The only important fact she could impart was that his use of English was structurally good and that he didn't have a noticeable dialect. After an hour or so of fruitless attempts to get a face on paper I gave up, dismissed her gently, and pitched the drawing into the wastebasket. Handing her my business card I said, "Be sure to call us if you remember anything else."

Standard formula. She never called again. And as far as I know I never saw her again.

The following July a student I knew slightly was startled to see a medium-sized black male about thirty years old standing in the living room of the small house she shared with her sister in a neat middle-class neighborhood. Bonnie (pseudonym) had characteristically neglected to lock the door or lower the shades; the intruder had simply walked in after determining she was alone. He produced a handgun that, according to Bonnie, he fired once; he then ordered her outside and into the back yard, where a number of fruit trees threw dark shadows.

That is where the attack reportedly occurred.

I say reportedly because almost nothing about this case is clear. Once she had called the police and given her story, Bonnie refused to cooperate further. Although she saw the intruder in the well-lit living room, and in spite of the fact that I had known the girl for a long time, she refused to be interviewed for a drawing. Naturally reticent and grossly overweight, she withdrew even further and left town with her boyfriend, whom she married shortly thereafter.

The detectives never found the bullet the rapist supposedly fired, nor any indication of one, though they combed the dwelling thoroughly. They saw two possibilities: either Bonnie's imagination was working overtime, or, in the moment of panic, she failed to realize that he had fired the gun outside not inside.

However she did note that, as in the April incident, the attacker's use of English was in a standard dialect. Because everything else matched—size, age, coloration, toboggan cap and M. O., including firing his gun once, apparently for effect—it appeared more than likely that the same man was the offender in both cases.

But we were no nearer to a solution than before. We had no idea what the perp really looked like. A good forensic drawing would help a lot.

We already had a drawing of sorts dating back to 3 April, when a city employee named Gordon Pettey returned home to find a medium-sized black male standing in the center of his living room.

"What the hell are you doing here?" Pettey asked, starting toward the intruder.

The man produced a gun that Pettey described as an automatic and fired one shot at the ceiling, then bolted out the back way without a word, but not before Pettey had gotten a good look at him.

I met Pettey at the P.D. and found him to be both articulate and intelligent. A member of the city planning office, he was in line for a significant post in the city administration. Angered by the intrusion into his home, he was anxious to help us.

As the face he described began to take shape on paper, I became gradually aware of his growing frustration. It wasn't right. "The cheeks need to puff out," he said, "like those squirrels you see in Disney cartoons."

This is the point we never resolved because, without either of us being aware of it, we had hit a semantic impasse. By cheeks I assumed he meant the space between the zygomatic arch and the lower mandible, that is, the side of your face that puffs out like that of a pack rat when you put too much food in your mouth. But Pettey meant the front space over the malar bone between the eye socket and the upper teeth. Consequently, the more he instructed me to "make his cheeks fuller," the more I added space to the wrong area. After a while the image was downright grotesque and getting worse.

Finally I threw the drawing away and started over. The result was not much better, but we decided to go with it anyway because it was probably better than nothing. With great misgivings I turned the sketch over to the detectives, who had it multicopied and distributed (see Illustration No. 39).

It turned out to look almost nothing like Mike White. I include it here only because it demonstrates an axiom of police art that can't be repeated too often: the artist must be certain he and the witness are using a given term to mean the same thing; otherwise the two will end up talk-

Black male
23-25 yrs
170-180 lbs
5'6" - 5'8"
Distinguishing features:
1. Extremely square jaw
2. Full rounded cheeks
3. Young complexion unblemished
4. Dark skin
5. No visible scars

ILLUSTRATION NO. 39 Totally unrealistic sketch of suspect suprised in Pettey's house. It was without investigative value.

ing at cross purposes and the resultant drawing will probably be worthless. If Pettey had only pointed with his finger and said, "I mean here, not there," the result might have been a lot better.

Then, on 20 November 1983, Lieutenant Ernie Antle and Patrolman Gary Crabtree responded to a burglary-in-progress call on Central Avenue, across town. When the resident of the house, middle-aged Garnet Fletcher, first heard noises on her porch she ran to the second floor to get her gun, but when she came down and heard someone kicking in the front door she wisely decided to run out the back to the home of a neighbor, where she phoned the police.

The response of the two officers was classical and correct. Antle cut his lights off and parked fifty yards to the north of the Fletcher house, Crabtree went around the corner to the south. Crabtree moved to cover the rear of the building. As Antle moved to the front he heard a shot inside. He was later to learn that White had apparently seen Crabtree's silhouette through a window and fired at it, striking a clothes dryer. Before Antle could move more than a few feet the door burst open and a man later identified as Mike White tumbled onto the sidewalk. He twisted onto his side and fired twice, striking Antle in the foot. Fortunately the bullet only ruined a good shoe and raised a big blood blister as it grazed a toe. Antle returned fire and heard White cry out "Oh shit!" He chased White and continued to fire until his revolver was empty, at which point White fired more shots at Antle. One of them grazed his jacket. Central Avenue is poorly lighted in that area, and as Antle slowed to reload, White, though badly wounded, was able to escape by running between some houses.

In doing so, White passed a window where he was seen at close range by a young woman who, hearing the shots, had raised her shade to see what was going on. She hailed the policemen and told them in very broken English that a man had run past her apartment holding his stomach and "making a noise of hurting." Antle and Crabtree had difficulty understanding her but gathered she could describe the man. They radioed the station to phone me.

Sunily Manrique, recently arrived from Venezuela, could barely make her wants known in English, let alone describe a face to a police artist. We went immediately to Spanish, and I discovered that her speech was not the language of the grandees but a patois comparable in elegance and precision to the English of a Brooklyn cabdriver or a Limehouse fishwife. Nevertheless she was helpful and anxious to please, and between the two of us we produced a couple of sketches, one in straight profile and one three-quarter view. (She never saw him full-face.) I turned the straight profile in to the investigators. It has since disappeared from Mike White's file, presumably at the time of White's trial, though nobody at the courthouse has any record of it. I kept the three-quarter view, which is included here (Illustration No. 40), along with a mug shot of White (Illustration No. 41).

As it turned out, the drawing was not necessary to identify White. Although he had been able to make it back to his rented car, he was forced to seek medical help at a hospital in southern Ohio. His two bullet wounds were quickly reported, and as soon as he recovered he was taken to jail.

The trial would have taken less time, and proof would have been more conclusive, had the State been able to es-

Courtesy of Franklin County, Ohio
Sheriff's Department

ILLUSTRATION No.41   Mug shot of Mike White.

ILLUSTRATION   No.40   Three-quarter   view   of
Mike White.

tablish that the bullets still in Mr. White's body came from Lieutenant Antle's gun. The prosecution tried to get a court order to have them removed so they could be submitted along with the revolver to Ohio's Bureau of Criminal Investigation for scientific comparison; but the court refused on the ground that the U.S. Supreme Court had already ruled in a similar case that such removal would violate the Constitutional guarantee against unreasonable searches and seizures. White could therefore keep Antle's bullets within his body for as long as it pleased him. The prosecution, for its part, felt that if there is probable cause to believe one has collected some hot lead in the course of violent criminal behavior, freely undertaken, then there is nothing unreasonable about recovery of that lead through humane surgical procedures. But the prosecution proposes and the court disposes.

In any case, it turned out to be unnecessary. There was ample evidence—blood samples taken from the rented car and the pavement, eyewitnesses, White's handwriting on the auto rental agreement, etc.—to place him at the scene of the crime and in transit to the hospital. He was convicted with relative ease, at least on the Central Avenue incident. He has not been tried on the others because there is simply insufficient evidence. However, the descriptions given by the rape victims, by Gordon Pettey, by Sunily Manrique, and by others are remarkably consistent: black male approaching 30; medium height and weight; use of standard English; dark skin; roundish face; and the use of a handgun. In three of the cases he fired one shot for effect. It is therefore not surprising to professional law officers that the crime wave bearing a particular trademark, or M.O., came to a halt when White was captured.

CHAPTER 12

Of Courage, Cowardice and Coincidence

Most people think they know their own psychological makeup well enough to predict with some accuracy how they would respond to different challenges. To a certain degree they may be right, but when those challenges involve a threat to personal safety, or the safety of a loved one, all bets are off. The police artist encounters his share of surprises in this area, and when that happens the result can range from deep satisfaction to maddening frustration.

On 17 June 1986 Barry Lewis (pseudonym), a salesman for a Columbus supply firm, stopped at a rest area between Nelsonville and Logan just inside the Athens county line. As he exited his car he saw a stocky white male loitering nearby. When he came out of the men's rest room the unidentified male approached him, displayed a hunting knife, and ordered him to his car.

"Don't yell or I'll stick you," he said as he climbed in the passenger side. "Just drive 'til I say stop."

When they came to a side road he ordered Barry to pull over. "Give me your money," he said. Barry produced his wallet, which contained only twenty dollars.

"Is this all you got?"

"Yes."

The robber, angered, punched Barry about the eyes and mouth. Barry could taste blood as his assailant threw the empty wallet out the window. He then took Barry's watch, worth about seventy-five dollars, and beat him some more about the face, inflicting several severe cuts.

"Get out and lie down. You move and I'll run over you."

Barry did not need to be told twice. As he lay at the edge of the road he saw his assailant roar off to Route 33, make a right, and fishtail southeast. Arising, he dabbed his bleeding face and limped back to the highway. He was spotted by a state trooper and taken to the hospital, where they stitched him up.

I met Barry at the sheriff's office. A fat and pasty young man in his mid-twenties, he did not look able to punch his way out of a paper bag and was undoubtedly very wise not to resist. His lips were bruised and swollen and his face was swathed in neat white bandages. He had difficulty enunciating, but he wanted to get started on the drawings.

"Do you feel up to it just now?" I asked.

"Oh, yes. My face hurts, but I want to try. I can give you a very good description. I want him caught." His eyes were flashing pure anger.

"You'll prosecute?"

"Of course. I want to see him in jail. Look what he did to me. He didn't have to . . . I mean, I already gave him the money. . . ."

We set to work. At the end of an hour we had completed a full-face sketch (Illustration No. 42). "Do you want to do a side view too?" Barry asked. "I have

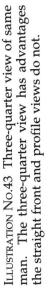

ILLUSTRATION No.42 Front view of knife- wielding robber from description by victim.

ILLUSTRATION No.43 Three-quarter view of same man. The three-quarter view has advantages the straight front and profile views do not.

plenty of time, if you do. I just want to help. I want the guy in jail."

Another forty-five minutes produced a three-quarter view (Illustration No. 43). As I was picking up to leave I said to him, "If we can locate this bird are you willing to drive down from Columbus to identify him?"

"Absolutely."

"You'll testify?"

"Absolutely."

I showed the drawings to the sheriff and two of his investigators. They looked at one another knowingly.

"Remind you of anybody?" I asked.

"Hell yes. That looks like Bubba Walker" (pseudonym).

"I thought he was in jail."

"He got out last week. That's his style. The whole thing's got his trademark stamped on it. And the picture looks just like him."

The following day they found Barry's car in the river, and they picked up Bubba Walker loitering around a gas station on the south end of town. I was in the sheriff's office when they brought him in. As they led him past me I was astounded at the accuracy of Barry's description. The resemblance, especially in the three-quarter view, was close to photographic.

At that very moment the door opened and Barry Lewis walked in. Bubba Walker had been taken into an anteroom with a large glass window where he could be veiwed from the side. Barry took one look and gasped; the flicker of recognition was unmistakable. I have never seen anyone turn ashen so fast.

"Oh my God!"

"That him?" the sheriff asked.

Barry hesitated, his eyes darting.

"No," he said quickly. "No."

He turned on his heel and half-ran out the door. He never came back; as far as I know, he never even called.

The converse of that scenario occurred about a year earlier up in Logan. A young housewife named Wendy Robinson (pseudonym) made the most basic of all mistakes: she let a stranger into her house. Robert Embrey, who had a history of sex offenses, knocked on the door of her rural home one spring afternoon when Wendy's husband was at work and asked to use the phone. "My truck's broke down out there," he said, pointing to a pickup by the side the road.

Wendy hesitated, but admitted him. As soon as he was inside he pulled a pocket knife.

"Get your clothes off," he said. "Here. Now."

Terrified, with the knife pointed directly at her, she began to undress.

"Hurry up," the intruder said.

Her fingers trembling, she fumbled with buttons and zippers and let the clothes fall in a heap. She was down to her underpants.

"Take 'em off," he commanded. "Everything."

She obeyed.

At that point Embrey began removing his own clothing, an item at a time. Wendy began to get an idea. Though a tiny woman (she weighed perhaps ninety-five pounds) she had no intention of giving in without a scrap, especially to some sawed-off slimeball who just walked in off the road. When he had removed everything but his underpants she did what she had never thought about doing, had never even dreamed she was capable of doing.

She kicked him in the crotch as hard as she could.

As he doubled over in pain she darted out the front door and ran, naked as the day she was born, to the home of a neighbor where she phoned the sheriff. By the time deputies arrived Embrey had disappeared.

I was at the Athens P.D. when the call came in from Logan. Wendy was waiting when I got there, anxious to get started. I had to admire this gutsy little spitfire who had outsmarted and driven off a rapist armed with a knife. Her husband, who was present, was clearly proud of his little wife and very supportive of her.

The girl was bright, observant, self-confident. She knew what she had seen, she could describe things clearly and she didn't hesitate to tell me when my lines or shadows needed to be corrected. Her description, with certain minor discrepancies, was close enough so that a parole officer to whom the drawing was shown recognized Embrey as one of his own boys. Embrey was behind bars again within thirty-six hours (Illustration No. 44).

Repeatedly in this book we have noted the impact— often terrifying, sometimes dramatic, not infrequently pathetic—that crime has on its victims. Wendy's courage under fire was prodigious, and we can only admire it. Yet when the incident was over, when the drawing was complete, her emotions took over and swept away the facade of self-assurance. With a sudden cry she threw herself into her husband's arms.

"I don't want to go back to that house," she sobbed. "I want to go home again. Take me back to Missouri, please." I tiptoed out as she sat on her husband's lap, crying silently.

I am sure Wendy was never happy in that house again. I don't know if they stayed or left; but in either case the neighborhood was changed, and the lives of

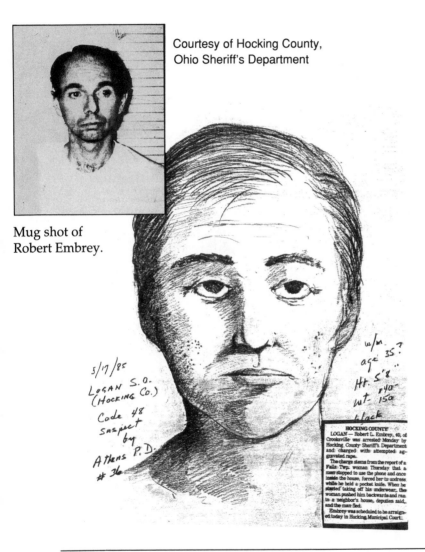

Courtesy of Hocking County,
Ohio Sheriff's Department

Mug shot of
Robert Embrey.

5/17/85
LOGAN S.O.
(HOCKING Co.)
Code 48
suspect
by
Athens P.D.
36

w/m ?
age 35?
Ht 5'8"
wt 140
150
black

HOCKING COUNTY
LOGAN — Robert L. Embrey, 40, of Crooksville was arrested Monday by Hocking County Sheriff's Department and charged with attempted aggravated rape.

The charge stems from the report of a Falls Twp. woman Thursday that a man stopped to use the phone and once inside the house, forced her to undress while he held a pocket knife. When he started taking off his underwear, the woman pushed him backwards and ran to a neighbor's house, deputies said, and the man fled.

Embrey was scheduled to be arraigned today in Hocking Municipal Court.

ILLUSTRATION No. 44 Convicted sex offender Robert Embrey. He was captured on the basis of this sketch within 36 hours of an attempted rape.

Wendy and her husband were changed. As for Wendy, she may not have been raped in the technical sense, but she will never be the same.

Gertrude Spears (pseudonym) made a similar mistake: she stopped to ask directions without locking the door. Gertrude and her husband had just moved down from Cleveland. A country boy to begin with, he was anxious to get back to the land; but Gertrude, a city girl, was not accustomed to it and had difficulty adjusting. Large-framed and somewhat overweight, there was about her a city-bred softness that didn't accord well with rough rural living. She might have been at home on expressways and crowded thoroughfares, but on rural back roads she was close to helpless.

She managed to get lost one summer evening on the way home from a nearby village. As she topped a rise at the intersection of two dirt roads she saw a youth walking in the same direction. Pulling abreast, she said, "I'm sort of lost. Can you tell me how to get to. . . ."

That was as far as she got before the youth yanked open the door of her small pickup truck and pulled a small knife. With his free hand he dragged her from the cab and slammed her up against the side of the vehicle. Raising her skirt, he jabbed at the inside of her thighs with the point of his knife, cutting her. Although he continued to rough her up, there was some question as to whether he actually accomplished forcible penile penetration. In any case he left her a hysterical wreck. Somehow she found her way home, though by that time it was dark. Her husband drove her to the hospital, where she was treated and released.

I did not get to interview her for almost three days because she refused to leave her home. She just sat inside and cried. On the third day her husband and a sheriff's deputy convinced her to try to talk with me, and brought her in about 7:00 P.M.. It turned out to be one of my more difficult interviews.

The poor woman was completely devastated. Her face was drawn and tear-stained, her mouth trembled, her whole frame shook. At first she was unable even to reply yes or no to simple questions without dissolving into wracking sobs. For a while I considered giving up and telling her husband to bring her in later when she had time to get control of herself. On the other hand it occurred to me that if she left we might never get her to come back. I decided to wing it as best I could.

"Look, Mrs. Spears," I said. "I'm not going to ask you to talk at all until you're ready. I'm just going to ask some questions. If the answer is yes, just nod. If it's no just shake you're head. It's going to be like that old game of Twenty Questions. Okay?"

She nodded.

I began by showing her my chart of head shapes. By using the yes-or-no approach, we got around to the heart shape. From there I went to the negative spaces, which worked fine because I could use the bracketing method (wider? narrower? etc.) until we came to the space between the hairline and the eyebrows.

"I . . . I couldn't see," she said in a barely audible voice. "He was wearing a cap."

Words. I exchanged glances with her husband, who looked encouraged. At least she had said something, but almost immediately she started to cry again and I had to wait for her to regain control.

So it went, a half-step at a time, an agonizingly slow process interrupted repeatedly by spates of crying, or worse yet, total silence.

Nevertheless a face was taking shape as Mrs. Spears began to talk more. She was able to help me by telling me when something was wrong, but often could not tell me how to correct it. There was something about the set of the cheeks that bothered her.

I decided to try a sharp shadow at the top of the malar bone. The effect was electric.

"My God! That's *him!*" Mrs. Spears turned to her husband, sobbing. "It's him! It's him!" He had to console his wife for a good ten minutes while I went for Major Bob Dougherty, who was handling the investigation. When I came back I saw that Mr. Spears was undergoing some sort of emotional crisis, clamping his teeth, clenching and unclenching his fists, breathing audibly through distended nostrils. I took him by the elbow and led him into the hall.

"I'm pretty sure I know who that is," he told me. "I'm going to go get him and beat him to death with my bare fists." Mr. Spears was a young strong farmer, a good hundred eighty pounds of lean hard muscle, and he was mad enough to use it all.

"Don't even think about it," I told him. I don't know how long I talked to him—perhaps fifteen minutes, maybe longer—but I remember telling him that if he beat up his wife's attacker it would be he, not the attacker, who would go to jail.

"Your pretty wife needs you," I told him. "What good are you going to be to her if you're locked up? Sure, it would feel great to smash the guy's face, but then what? All you'll have is some broken knuckles and a jail record."

After a while he calmed down, but I was by no means

sure he wouldn't flare up again.

The deputies took the drawing (Illustration No. 45) out into the area of the attack and showed it around among the neighbors. Five out of seven identified him as the grandson of a local farmer. The boy had a record of sex offenses, including piqueurism, an abberation in which the offender derives sexual gratification by jabbing the flesh of a victim with sharp instruments.

The alleged offender was picked up and brought in for questioning. He denied any knowledge of the offense and agreed to take a polygraph test, which he passed.

I believe giving him the test was a tactical error because, despite the claims of manufacturers and certified operators of polygraphs, they *can* be beaten, and often are, by psychopaths. This happens because, in many instances, such people actually believe their own fabrications, with the result that their bodies do not manifest the changes registered on a polygraph when a normal person tells a lie.

Be that as it may, the polygraph test results shot down the prosecution's case. Chalk another up for the bad guys.

Elaine Scarlett is one of the best witnesses I have ever interviewed. Intelligent, straightforward and soft-spoken, she exudes an air of quiet self-confidence and emotional control. In 1983 she was a teller at the Tri-County bank in Coolville, Ohio. She was on duty the morning of 16 November when a fairly tall white male wearing a hooded sweat shirt and a stocking mask entered the bank, produced a gun, and made off with an undisclosed amount of cash, none of which was marked and was therefore untraceable.

Actually, she was one of two tellers on duty. The

Illustration No. 45   Rape suspect who was I.D.'d by five people from this sketch but who beat the polygraph.

other was Patty Hand, a young woman in her late twenties. Mrs. Hand was the one I interviewed first, largely by chance. The drawing from Mrs. Hand's description is included here, for purposes of comparison, though it is somewhat unrealistic and from the beginning did not inspire confidence. Mrs. Hand seemed more inclined to report intangibles such as impressions, attitudes, and her personal value judgments based on aesthetic considerations. The robber's nose, for example was "cute." Now I can draw a straight nose, or a broken nose, or a Roman or button or hook nose, but I have to know what you mean by cute before I can apply the concept to a pictorial rendition of somebody's schnozzle. Since Mrs. Hand and I never did hammer out the linear equivalents of her descriptive terminology, the drawing based on her reportage got shelved right off the bat (Illustration No. 46).

Mrs. Scarlett, however, favored precision in her choice of words. The offender's nose was straight, his chin was round, his face was oval, etc. In about an hour I had a drawing that she classified as a highly accurate rendition of the man she remembered seeing. I took the sketch back and showed it to Sheriff Allen, who had a way of coming directly to the point while dispensing with unnecessary verbiage:

"Why, I just talked to that sumbitch!"

The suspect was one Earl Ingles Jr., and he came from the area near the Tri-County Bank. His mug shot is shown here together with the drawing from Mrs. Scarlett's description (Illustration No. 47). Whatever his guilt or lack of it, one can perceive a strong resemblance between the two images.

The reasons he became a suspect (aside from the drawing) were several. First, a credible witness saw a

ILLUSTRATION NO. 46 From Patty Hand's description of the Tri-county bank robber.

Courtesy of Athens County, Ohio Sheriff's Department

ILLUSTRATION NO. 47 Sketch from Elaine Scarlett's description of the same man. Note comparison with mug shot of Ingles (left), who was found innocent.

man matching Ingles' height and build emerge from the bank holding a bag. The man, who was wearing a sweat suit and a stocking over his face, got into a black Ford truck and drove away. The witness took down the license number and gave it to the police. The truck was soon found abandoned about a half mile from Coolville; it was traced to a local car dealership from which it had disappeared the night before the robbery. Ingels, it was asserted, had examined the vehicle that day, 15 November, and had borrowed the keys to test drive it with possible purchase in mind. When he returned the vehicle fifteen minutes later, only one of the two keys fit. The truck was gone the next morning and Ray Riggs, owner of the car dealership, immediately reported it stolen.

As soon as Ingles was certain he was a suspect, he took refuge in West Virginia and declined to be extradited. West Virginia did not cooperate with Ohio in the matter, and Ingles could have remained free indefinitely if he had not slipped across the river to an apartment he maintained in Cincinnati. There he was arrested.

Ingles' attorney was one Thomas Eslocker, who has amassed much experience in criminal defense and serves as legal advisor to a tabloid with a history of gentle treatment for mischief-makers and correspondingly severe scrutiny of law enforcement. Tom, who is a very personable guy, did an artful job of knocking these facts down like ducks in a shooting gallery. He demonstrated for the jury that the keys *could* have been stolen by somebody else; that the truck *could* have been hot-wired without a trace of tampering; that the apparently new clothing and furniture in Ingles' apartment at the time of his arrest *could* have been old but well-cared for; that the theft of the truck just before the robbery *could* have been coincidence;

and that Ingles' flight to West Virginia *could* have been motivated by fear of being framed.

But the star defense witness was Ingles' mother. She took the stand to testify that the new furniture in her son's apartment was in fact over a year old; that as far as she knew he had never owned a pistol; that she and her son Earl enjoyed a particularly warm mother-son relationship; that he had been at home sleeping at 11:00 A.M., under the loving eye of his mother, when the offense occurred; and that in the first place she, Bessie Ingles, didn't raise her son to be a bank robber. You could hear the violins.

The jury did everything but award Ingles the key to the city.

The legal process has found him innocent of the Tri-County Bank robbery, and that is what he is presumed to be: innocent.

For that reason we must conclude that the startling resemblance between the mug shot and the drawing, like everything else, *could* be coincidence. The only thing the sketch really accomplishes is to demonstrate that nylon stockings are more effective on women's legs than on robbers' faces.

CHAPTER 13

People Do the Craziest Things

For most of us, it is impossible to imagine being so desperate for attention that we would walk into a police station and confess to a murder we didn't commit, in the mad hope of seeing, for once in our lives, our name or photo in the newspaper.

But it happens. When it does, the police have no trouble dismissing such pitiful creatures. Because most if not all of their information about the crime comes from the news media in the first place, they know only the bare outline. A couple of quick questions based on details known only to the police usually suffice to send the would-be gallows birds on their pathetic way.

However, the police often have to deal with another type of falsehood: the report of a crime that never occurred. This is something that can waste a *lot* of time.

There are many motivations for such false reports. Insurance fraud is one. In a recent Virginia case, police and insurance investigators spent months on a reported jewelry theft, only to find the missing gems sealed up behind a false wall in the owner's home, where she planned to keep them until the company paid off. The number of man-hours misspent on that investigation represents a sizeable sum chargeable, one way or another, to the citizenry. In the opinion of this writer, the owner of the jewels ought to be ordered to reimburse the county and the insurance company for the wages of the detectives.

In many cases, though, it's simply not worth the effort to try to collect because the filer of the false report doesn't have the price of a square meal.

Domestic cases are a good example. Charges and counter-charges between spouses who no longer love each other can range from simple harassment to assault to child stealing to attempted murder. Sometimes these people will carry out a bluff to the extent of describing a totally fictitious person to a police artist. When that happens it is very frustrating, especially when you're taken away from something important, or a good night's sleep.

Two-Ton Tessie was a case in point. She had another name, which I have forgotten. She lived alone except for a school age daughter (her husband had decamped), and she made a living as a hairdresser. She called the police with some regularity, which, given the area where she lived, was not surprising. It was a housing development consisting of rows of half-timbered town houses, originally designed for a young working clientele. Like so many such projects, it had quickly been taken over by HUD recipients long on children and short on cash. The result was a faubourg of broken windows, noisy jalopies and spray-painted graffiti; of Saturday nights punctuated by the thuds, bumps and yells of domestic squabbles; and of fetid air perfumed by the heavy odors of garbage dumpsters and marijuana smoke. Thievery was rife, dope dealing was common, and police routinely answered all calls to that area in pairs.

On 13 May 1986, close to midnight, Two-Ton Tessie phoned to report she had just been robbed at knife point. Hearing noises, she had come downstairs to be confronted by a large black male brandishing what she described as a twelve-inch butcher knife. When she could not produce the cash he demanded, he helped himself to a loaf of bread and some other goodies from her refrigerator and left. She could describe him very well.

Her story had some serious holes in it, but burglary and armed robbery are felonies and you can't just ignore them. There had been other such incidents in the neighborhood; a police sketch was in order.

The dispatcher woke me up about 1:00 A.M. I rode out to Tessie's place in a cruiser with a uniformed patrolman who had worked investigations and was a pretty good photographer. I would do the sketch while he dusted for prints and shot some film.

It was one of my less aesthetic experiences. Two-Ton Tessie billowed over the sides of her chair in great rolls of fat that jiggled under a sleazy chenille bathrobe dotted with food stains. You could pardon her surplus tonnage on the ground that perhaps she couldn't help it, but there was another problem: she stank. I don't mean a mild case of B.O. that can result from sudden fear; I mean the woman hadn't bathed in God knows how long. Moreover, prior to my arrival she had eaten something heavily seasoned with garlic. When you do a police sketch the witness must sit next to you or stand looking over your shoulder, so as to monitor progress. I found myself holding my breath as I tried to work.

The drawing (Illustration No. 48) is highly improbable: the hair mushrooms out from the sides of the head in a style you don't see in contemporary black males. I

ILLUSTRATION NO. 48 Anonymous knife-point robber of Two-Ton Tessie.

questioned it, but Two-Ton Tessie—who was, after all, a hairdresser—insisted that was the way he wore it. She was also quite precise about a couple of other details: very large, flaring ears and a small gold earring in the right one. I left with mixed feelings about the reality of the intruder; I was just glad to get out in the fresh air.

Some months later, on 13 October, Tessie called again and claimed to have been raped by two men: one white, one black. I could not quite imagine any male of normal sensibilities getting close enough to Tessie to commit rape, but as in the previous case, a felony is a felony and you have to investigate.

Once again, she could give descriptions. She thought it possible that the black man was the same one who had robbed her at knife point the previous May. She did not think she had seen the white man before, but described details such as acne scars with enough precision to suggest a certain credibility (see Illustrations No. 49 and 50). However, she had refused the routine rape examination at the hospital as well as the assistance of rape-crisis counsellor Cheryl Cesta-Miller, Care Line or anyone else. She merely waddled into the police station to file a report.

I was there when she appeared. By that time I had piled up a fair amount of experience with rape victims, and I didn't see any of the signs of stress or trauma, either emotional or physical, usually associated with forcible rape. As she flopped into the chair next to me I perceived no closer acquaintance with soap and water than she had shown the first time. I went through the motions of drawing the alleged offenders, but after she left I told the investigators I had my doubts they even existed.

It turned out I was right. At one time Tessie had a husband, who left her for reasons I don't find terribly sur-

Code 48
86 - 7946
Suspect No. 1
10/13/86

By #36

ILLUSTRATION No. 49 One of two anonymous rapists of Two-Ton Tessie.

By #36

Code 48
86-7946
Suspect No. 2
10/13/86

ILLUSTRATION No. 50 White male companion of Two-Ton Tessie's alleged rapist. She claimed he participated in the offense.

prising. In some twisted way, she thought that if she could project an image of danger to herself and her daughter, his protective instincts would cause him to return. She hoped the incidents she reported would get enough media coverage to send him a clear message. Pathetically, it didn't work.

False reporting of a crime is, of course, a crime in itself. People like Tessie generally aren't charged and prosecuted because it would waste both prosecutorial time and jail space on offenders who are more nutty than evil. In addition, public defenders would put as much time into proving that the alleged crime did occur as they normally spend trying to prove it didn't. In most cases it's just not worth the bother.

Occasionally someone who fabricates a crime and attempts to describe a fictitious offender will end up describing himself instead. One summer morning in 1987 the dispatcher phoned me before dawn to say that there had been a rape and that the victim, who was at the station, was ready to give a description to me. I had been up fairly late the night before and sort of wished for a bit more sleep before starting a sketch. Nevertheless I shoved my feet through pants legs, pulled on a T-shirt and drove uptown, yawning.

When I opened the station door I saw a lone individual in the waiting area, sitting disconsolately on a wooden bench in the glare of the overhead fluorescent light. Sad-eyed and aggrieved, he was obviously what is known in police circles and elsewhere as a "queen"—that is, a male homosexual who affects the speech and mannerisms of women.

He claimed to have been forcibly raped by an unknown and unarmed male. My skepticism quotient rose by several points because the man I was looking at was squat and thick, muscular not soft, and he weighed perhaps two hundred pounds. I figured that if he did not wish to be raped, any lone unarmed male short of, say, King Kong would have his troubles doing it.

But we proceeded with the drawing anyway. Before long I began doing double takes at the sketch and at the face of my witness. Curiously enough, the resemblance was becoming progressively more striking. By the time I finished, only the hair style was different; otherwise it could have been a portrait of the teary-eyed individual before me.

I turned the drawing in to the investigators. "I don't think any rape occurred," I said. "I don't know what this guy's game is, but he's feeding us bullshit. I'm going back and get some sleep."

The investigators questioned him and learned that, in fact, no rape had taken place at all. The complainant and his current boyfriend had had a lover's quarrel. My witness decided to get even by reporting a felony in the hope the police would give his roommate a good scare, if nothing else. But in describing the supposed offender, he ended up describing himself. There is no point in prosecuting someone like that. One of the detectives sent him back to the apartment he shared with his lover.

"Go kiss and make up," the detective told him. "Next time I'll charge you with giving false information" (see Illustration No. 51).

On another occasion a teenage girl reported being harassed on a country road by a man about thirty-five. According to the girl, the subject pulled abreast of her in his car and attempted to persuade her to get in. When she refused he kept insisting as he slowed his vehicle to a

Code 48-H
SUSPECT

Age 40
5'9"
200#
Muscular

no scars,
warts or
moles

ILLUSTRATION No. 51 Sketch of alleged homosexual rapist. Aside from the hair, this the spitting image of the alleged victim.

walk. Frightened, she broke into a run. The subject caught her and struck her several times, though she did not report any sexual molestation.

There were several serious weaknesses to her story. For one, she did not bother to note the license number of the vehicle, nor the make or model, nor the color or condition of the interior, though she had ample opportunity to do so. Also, she bore no bruises or other evidence of physical abuse. Whether she did this to frighten her mother, to concoct an excuse for being late after school or merely to tell a good story is unclear, and it doesn't really matter. The important thing is that the mother became alarmed, especially because the girl's school bus discharged her at that spot daily. She insisted that the girl come with her to the sheriff's office to make a report.

In over her head, the kid clearly did not wish to be there. Further, she obviously did not expect the chief investigator to call in a police artist. But because law enforcement agencies in that area take offenses against children very seriously, and keep very close tabs on known or suspected offenders, she was forced either to continue the bluff or toss in her cards. She elected to bluff.

The face that appeared on the drawing pad is wholly unrealistic (Illustration No. 52). Although in this instance it does not look like the witness herself, it is patently the face of a woman, not a man. And although in this day British sailors are not the only males who wear earrings, the double heart dangling from the right lobe certainly does nothing to fortify our acceptance of her story.

The investigator made a wry face and shrugged. "I'll take care of it," he said.

I don't know if the girl succeeded in fooling her mother or not. Certainly she did not impress the cops. If

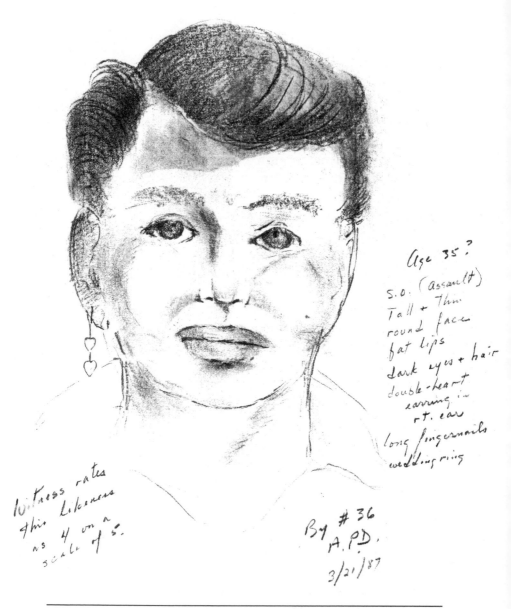

ILLUSTRATION No. 52 Improbable likeness of alleged child molester as given by a teen-age girl. There is considerable doubt the offense occurred.

in fact there was such a person as the girl described—which I seriously question—nobody else has seen him/her in that end of the county before or since.

What people such as this girl or Two-Ton Tessie fail to consider is the impact such deceptions have on the whole community, the police constabulary as well as other potential victims. It is bad enough to tie up public servants for hours, days, or weeks on a wild goose chase; far worse is the effect of crying wolf. For although the police will continue to respond to calls from a given address even when they know from experience they are probably false, the result is heightened frustration and diminution of enthusiasm. The call that comes over the radio from the dispatcher is brief, cryptic and to the point: "Code forty-six, 119 Calloway Lane." The comment that follows in the cruiser, after the acknowledgment has been made and the mike is closed, is equally to the point: "Shit! Ol' Crazy Jinnie is hearing bumps in the attic again. Just when we was gonna go eat." But even though Crazy Jinnie has called fifty times in the last six months, you still have to respond on the double because this time it could be for real—and God forbid you should get there too late.

You can forgive the Crazy Jinnies of this world because they are honestly in fear. It is somewhat harder to forgive the jokers who knowingly, for whatever reason, report crimes that never occurred.

One of the craziest cases I have encountered involved the theft of a $6,000 diamond ring.

One bright September morning in 1984 a young man walked into Cornwell's Jewelry and engaged one of the three sales clerks in conversation about wristwatches. The other two clerks paid little attention, noting only this man's massive build and great muscularity. A sign painter, who was there only to collect his paycheck, saw nothing. In an earlier day the boy's appearance might have inspired considerable interest; but in a modern college community, where hordes of young Arnold Schwarzeneggers gobble steriods like peanuts at a cocktail party, such physiques are common.

After examining and rejecting several expensive watches, he turned his attention to rings. It seems he was very much in love and was contemplating marriage; perhaps his money would be better invested in an engagement ring. Could he see some diamonds?

The clerk brought a tray of expensive rings from the safe and placed it on the counter for his inspection. He scrutinized two or three with apparent care. At that point a telephone rang, distracting the clerk's attention. The customer simply picked up one of the rings, pocketed it, and walked out into the crowd of morning shoppers.

I was called almost immediately. Later that day, at the P. D., I met with the first witness, an attractive young woman who prefers anonymity. It was difficult to interview her because she was on the point of tears, her voice quavered when she tried to talk, and her hands shook uncontrollably. Her fear of being fired for carelessness was second only to her feelings of guilt and shame for allowing herself to be victimized.

My witness was not the cry-baby type; she was competent, intelligent and strong willed. Yet she was devastated in the same way, though perhaps not to the same degree, that she would have been by rape instead of larceny. It occurred to me that if the offender were caught, the charge of larceny would only address the fact of the actual theft, which amounted to $6,000. By its very nature, this charge would ignore the more serious offense—

the psychological trauma inflicted on the victim—on which no price can be placed.

The drawing from this girl's description appears as Illustration No. 53. She was unsure of it, did not trust her memory, and described it as unsatisfactory.

The second witness was a woman approaching middle age who chose not to cooperate; she said she was polishing glassware when the young man was in the store and hardly noticed him. Although she made two appointments with me, she reneged on both. It was perhaps just as well; she appeared so brittle she would doubtless have cracked like a china teacup in any kind of interview.

The third witness was a very level-headed woman in her mid-thirties who was willing to spend whatever time was necessary. The drawing from this description appears as Illustration No. 54. Surprisingly, there are areas of startling resemblance between this image and No. 53, despite the first witness' doubts about her own memory.

One would think that a boy of such proportions—six feet three, 250 pounds, massively muscular, with dark wavy hair and even white teeth—would be easy to spot around a college of some fifteen thousand students. Not so. At least two dozen such people surfaced within hours. Interrogation of the most likely suspects revealed nothing. I even did a third drawing, based on further informal conversations with the two witnesses who cooperated (Illustration No. 55). It served only to produce another suspect who was dismissed as being too small.

Then, two days later, the ring showed up again. It was mailed back to Cornwell Jewelers in a small package that had been certified for special handling at the Athens Post Office, not a mile away.

Investigators interviewed three post office employees

ILLUSTRATIONS No. 53, 54, 55: Front, profile and three-quarter views of diamond thief.

who had seen the young man at the window. In each case the reponse to the question, "What did he look like?" was simply, "I don't know. I wasn't looking," or "I didn't notice." That subject will be examined in the next chapter.

Police theorize that the theft was part of a fraternity initiation rite and that the thief believed that once the jewel was returned the account was more or less canceled. I have news for him: the police would still arrest him for the original charge, which remains larceny. Any leniency from the prescribed penalty would depend on the court.

CHAPTER 14
You're on Your Own

Throughout this book you have almost certainly noted that people see very little of what is right in front of them. Perhaps you have sensed, even shared, the frustration of an investigator who asks a simple question such as What did he look like? only to hear these stock replies:

> *I didn't notice.*
> *He had an average face.*
> *I ain't no camera, mister.*
> *I wasn't looking.*
> *Black people all look alike.*
> *White people all look alike.*
> *Chinamen all look alike.*
> *I was watching the gun, man.*
> *My mind was on something else.*
> *I was scared. I fainted already.*

When the investigator happens to be an artist whose business is to ferret out the precise details of a human face and put them together in a recognizable likeness—a tool of some utility in taking a dangerous felon off the streets—you can appreciate his urge to jump off a bridge.

Even trained police investigators, whose job depends on their powers of observation, are often unable to apply those powers to reporting what somebody actually looked like. That is partly because they have formed the habit of scanning an entire scene—reading the street, as it were. Thus a policeman will automatically seek information on:

— race, sex, age
— height, weight, build
— clothing: style, age, condition
— weapon(s), if any
— distinguishing marks, facial hair
— mannerisms, dialect, speech impediments
— vehicle, if any
— direction of travel.

When these essentials are settled, he may proceed to such things as complexion, attitudes, eyeglasses or jewelry. But when it comes to the face, he is likely to be as inept as any bank teller, gas station attendant or convenience store clerk who has just looked down a gun barrel.

If this seems surprising, consider some of the changes in our social and economic structures, our manners and mores, and our physical surroundings over the past half century. These changes have played beer and skittles with the way we look at the people and places around us.

Chief among these is technology. Years ago you figured out tomorrow's weather by the colors in the sunset and sunrise; you watched for rings around the moon and you knew what they meant; or you cocked your head as the freight train lumbered along the river, alert for that mournful note in the steam whistle that foretold rain. Nowadays we have television; we press a button and presto! we have a detailed satellite image depicting clouds in motion and predicting exactly where it will rain, how much, and when it will quit. Other factors also contribute to our atrophy.

Take manners, for example. In my youth, you looked at people you were talking with. If you didn't you got bawled out. ("Look at me, young man, when I'm talking to you!") Today, however, we are a lot more casual in our personal relationships. Perhaps that is for the best, because we are no doubt a lot more comfortable without the artificial restraints of Victorian pomposity. But once again, the change has affected our observational habits.

How many times in the past week have you dealt with somebody—bank teller, gas station attendant, store clerk, security guard—who never exchanged glances with you? Internationally known forger, imposter and con artist Frank Abagnale, author of *Catch Me if You Can*, once told me he was able to avoid capture for years because his victims so seldom looked at his face. They also occasionally failed to notice that some of his checks did not have even one perforated border—a dead giveaway to a piece of hot paper.

Still another factor in the rise of perceptual atrophy is the shift in public education away from attention to detail and memorization toward the holistic approach which stresses the overview.

Viewing the mountain of disarray, confusion and outright chaos that is the stuff of life, we begin to suspect that the mastery of observing it—or at least observing the portion of it that might be important to us at the moment—

lies in organization. Every field of human endeavor or scholarly interest—science, the arts, law, history, sports—depends on organization with a basic scheme that must be mastered by every neophyte. So why not observation?

Start with such an apparently limited thing as a single human being. Where is the most basic place to begin? *Features that cannot be changed.* This includes basic bone and muscle structure, which, in the absence of plastic surgery or major accidental disfigurement, is going to remain pretty constant throughout one's adult life.

Next, notice those features that can be changed, but only with time, effort or expense. Here we think especially of body weight, or of growing hair.

Then think of those items that can be changed easily, such as clothing; and finally those things that can be discarded altogether such as jewelry, eyeglasses, weapons, purses, briefcases, etc.

In a nutshell, when you set about describing somebody, the trick is to categorize what you need to remember *in descending order of importance.*

In the first chapter we referred to positive and negative spaces, which fall into our area of highest priority: things that cannot be changed. This notion is closely related to the critical distances on any human face. Once you have established in your mind the basic shape of the head, there are five relative distances between and surrounding the several features that generally can't be changed without destroying the resemblance.

Once you have decided what the offender's head shape reminds you of—such as a square, rectangle, or oval—you can complete your basic framework, not by trying to describe the individual features but by determining the relative distances between them. These are the distances to look for:

— from hairline to eyebrows
— from the inside corner of one eye to the
  inside corner of the other
— from the outside of one cheekbone to the
  outside of the other
— from the bottom of the nose to the top
  of the upper lip
— from the bottom of the lower lip to the
  bottom of the chin

The first of these is the distance from the hairline to the eyebrows. Many factors operate to alter this distance, either through reality (age, hair loss) or illusion (hair style) and for this reason it is the least dependable of all the critical distances. As a rule of thumb, prior to hair loss due to age, the hairline begins about halfway between the eyebrows and the crown.

A hairline significantly above this point may be called high; a hairline significantly below it can be called low.

We have said nothing about breadth of forehead because we don't need to. As the description progresses to include details such as hair style, widow's peak, "bachelor's forehead," etc., this distance will take care of itself. It is not critical in the sense that the height of the forehead is critical.

The second distance is that which lies across the bridge of the nose, between the eyes. This is basic to the makeup of a face. On the average, the length of one eye is the same as the distance between the eyes. If there is room left over, we say the eyes are wide-set; if there is not sufficient room for one eye between a person's eyes, we call them close-set.

The third critical distance is from the outside of one cheekbone to the outside of the other. Beginning just in front of each ear, and running forward to the eye socket, is the zygomatic arch, or cheekbone, which shows through the skin and throws a shadow across the middle and lower face. In some peoples, such as Eskimos and certain American Indians, this distance is much greater than in others. It is critical because it is unaffected by exterior distractors. Hair does not grow in this area, nor does fat accumulate here as it does in the neck and throat.

The fourth critical distance is perhaps the most important of all: the space between the bottom of the nose and the top of the upper lip. It is determined by the location and relative sizes of two bones: the nose bone and the upper jawbone or maxillary, which contains the sockets for the upper teeth. In some individuals it is very long; in others, quite short. In either case failure to note it can, and frequently does, result in a very inaccurate image in the mind of the witness.

As an example of how this works, let's consider former President Reagan. The distance between the bottom of his nose and the top of his upper lip is very long. The political cartoonists latch onto this feature and exaggerate it, so that in some extreme examples it appears to take up most of his face. This, together with a shock of hair perched on top of his cranium, tells us without words that we are looking at President Ronald Reagan and nobody else.

Now let's consider somebody with a short distance between nose and upper lip—Walter Mondale, for example. Do the cartoonists lengthen this distance as they do for President Reagan? On the contrary. What they do is shorten it even further. By exaggerating Mr. Mondale's tendency to shortness in this area, they give him an identity tag—a nutcracker face, in which the tip of the nose meets the point of the chin.

If the cartoonists were to reverse the procedure, giving Mr. Mondale President Reagan's Celtic upper jawbone and representing the former president's profile with the short upper jaw of his former rival, they would completely destroy the two likenesses.

That is precisely what happens when the viewer fails to note this extremely important distance.

The fifth critical distance is between the bottom of the lower lip and the bottom of the chin. Surprisingly, many people confuse the chin (properly speaking, the protrusion of the lower jawbone at the very front of the face) with the fold of fat directly below it seen in some obese persons. This latter is what we call a double chin and has nothing to do with critical distances. Still others confuse the terms chin and jaw. The result can be a ludicrous distortion of a human face, unless the detective or police artist takes the trouble to make sure he and the witness agree on the meanings of key words.

So how do you go about training yourself to notice these things? There are many techniques, but the best are those which make a game out of the procedure.

Any good program of self-training in observation will be based on two principles. The first is borrowed from speed reading. We learn to read by concentrating on each word as it appears—a habit that slows most readers to a rate not much faster than speaking. People who read faster than this have learned the simple trick of seeing several words at once. Some read a whole line at a time, and still others read more than one line, even a whole paragraph. They accomplish this by picking a point in the center of a line of print and training their eyes to expand the field of vision to both the left and the right. It takes time, and at first it is very frustrating, but in due course those who keep at it can see the whole line at once. A related skill, cultivated by those who read for the meat of the material, is that of culling out every word that gets in the way of the basic message, assigning priorities with computer-like speed.

The second principle is borrowed from pictures. When you read something, say a short story, you must absorb it in the order determined by the writer if it is to make any sense. But when you look at a picture in a book or gallery, you are free to start where you wish. You can "read" the picture, establishing your own order of priorities. That is fine as long as you have plenty of time. But when you are faced with a real-life picture on the street, where time is limited to seconds and things are in motion, you are forced into a speed-reading situation that leaves no chance for reflection. The person who has learned to expand his field of vision, like the speed reader, has a tremendous advantage.

So how do you go about this? First, you acknowledge that, like losing thirty pounds or mastering karate, it is not going to come to you overnight. It is going to require dedication and constant practice. Next, you get a loose-leaf notebook or a steno pad. Some people prefer to start with faces, others with things. A face is perhaps better because it allows you to concentrate on a small area. Choose somebody you know well.

Look directly at the bridge of the nose. Now, without shifting the focus, try to take in the general shape of the head. Think of some geometrical form it reminds you of, such as an oblong, triangle, square, or circle. Write this form on the left-hand side of the paper. Next, still focusing on the bridge of the nose, consider the five relative distances mentioned above. Classify each of these distances as long, medium or short, and write them on the right-hand side of the paper. You now have the basic framework for the whole face. Below, write a brief description of each major feature, including forehead, eyes, nose, mouth, chin and ears. Don't forget facial lines and hair style. Also, note any distinguishing marks.

Now pick out something you didn't notice before. This may be a scar, wart, mole, or any other disfigurement. You may be surprised. You have known this person for two years but never noticed that chipped tooth before.

At this point you are ready to go to the heart of all observation, which is that nothing is in perfect balance. That chipped tooth is not precisely in the center of the mouth. One side of the face will be heavier than the other. Other imbalances will surface on close inspection. One eye is higher than the other, perhaps. One ear is closer to the skull than the other, or the chin is a bit lopsided. Every human face has at least one area of imbalance, and most have several. You just have to look for them. Every face is different, like every set of fingerprints.

You have now finished page one of your notebook. Proceed to page two and repeat the exercise once again with someone you know well. Keep this up, one drawing a day, for a week.

By this time your consciousness level has been raised considerably. You are noticing all faces in greater detail, and your curiousity is aroused. Now repeat the same exercise with the faces of people you do not know. Do this carefully, a face a day, for another week.

Now put yourself under the clock. Up to this point you have had all the time you want. Begin with a time limit of thirty seconds and work down, five seconds per day, until you reach ten seconds. Alternate male and female faces. You should be able to see enough in ten seconds to give a very accurate description.

After you've been at it for three weeks and your notebook is growing, prepare your own questionnaire: a set of questions regarding a face or scene that will help you recall what you saw and organize your observations in a way that is meaningful to you. This is the point at which you shift to larger areas. You have a wide choice, but once again it is wise to begin with the familiar (your own neighborhood, for example) and work toward the unfamiliar. Proceed exactly as you did with faces, listing broad generalities on the left side of the paper and specifics on the right. Always look for things you didn't see before, and concentrate on imbalances. When you are ready, put yourself under the clock.

Go to a busy street corner, preferably one you don't know too well. Try to arrive when there are a lot of pedestrians and vehicle traffic. The first day you should give yourself plenty of time—fifteen or twenty seconds—to look in one direction, then leave promptly. Go some place where you can't see the corner and write down everything you can remember. Do this as soon after your viewing as possible. Gradually reduce the time exposure to the scene while increasing the time between the viewing and the writing until you can look for five seconds and write it down with all its essentials twenty-four hours later.

Does it sound impossible? Far from it. That is how the Spanish artist Francisco Goya produced the series of etchings he called *Disasters of War* in the days before photography.

Every face is as individual as every set of fingerprints. We presently have standards that specify the number of points that must match in a fingerprint to satisfy the legal requirements for an identity, but no such standards exist for faces. Until a system is developed, we are stuck with the testimony of eyewitnesses and the drawing done from such testimony by forensic artists.

You're on your own. You may never wish to become a police artist, but there's a good chance that in the course of your lifetime you will either witness a crime or be the victim of one.

If that should happen, remember that the police will want to know what the offender looked like, not what you think he might have been thinking. (Just the facts, ma'am.) An example of this occurred some years ago when an Irish lady pursuing doctoral studies in this country encountered an intruder in the hallway of the apartment building where she lived. In her charming brogue she spoke of his "sthrange athithude." "He had the appearance of some sorth of divil, with dape penethrating eyes that seemed to bore roight through ye." He seemed to be wondering what *she* was doing there; he stood looking at her like one of those haunting figures that rise, silent and accusing, from recently-dug graves. The drawing I did from the description is as vague and foreboding as the beautiful lady's words; it could be an illustration for a book of ghost stories (Illustration No. 56).

The intruder was seen at the same time and in the same hallway by a no-nonsense, streetwise young busi-

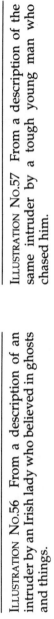

ILLUSTRATION No.57 From a description of the same intruder by a tough young man who chased him.

ILLUSTRATION No.56 From a description of an intruder by an Irish lady who believed in ghosts and things.

nessman from New York City, who challenged him and chased him down the street for a couple of blocks before losing him in a crowd of students. This man's description appears in Illustration No. 57. (Surprised?)

The battle against crime will continue as long as there are human beings to prey on one another. A particularly trenchant insight is provided by Richard Restak, M.D., in his fascinating best-seller *The Mind* (Bantam Books, 1988). Dr. Restak asks, If the human race can produce a Mother Teresa, whose fundamental goodness appears to spring from the soul rather than from any explanation based on science, can we not then postulate the existence of the spirit of evil in some people, equally independent of any genetic factors?

Good question.